D0327607

Falling North

IT'S IN THE HEARTACHE
- WE FIND THE JOY -

JOYELLE LEE

WESTBOW
PRESS®
A DIVISION OF THOMAS NELSON
& ZONDERVAN

Copyright © 2018 Joyelle Lee.
Interior Graphics/Art Credit: Faith Lee and Dianne Scafone.

All rights reserved. No part of this book may be used or reproduced by any means, graphic, electronic, or mechanical, including photocopying, recording, taping or by any information storage retrieval system without the written permission of the author except in the case of brief quotations embodied in critical articles and reviews.

This book is a work of non-fiction. Unless otherwise noted, the author and the publisher make no explicit guarantees as to the accuracy of the information contained in this book and in some cases, names of people and places have been altered to protect their privacy.

Unless otherwise indicated, all Scripture quotations are taken from the Holy Bible, New Living Translation, copyright © 1996, 2004, 2015 by Tyndale House Foundation. Used by permission of Tyndale House Publishers, Inc., Carol Stream, Illinois 60188. All rights reserved.

Scripture quotations marked (NIV) are taken from the Holy Bible, New International Version®, NIV®. Copyright © 1973, 1978, 1984, 2011 by Biblica, Inc.™ Used by permission of Zondervan. All rights reserved worldwide. www. zondervan.com The "NIV" and "New International Version" are trademarks registered in the United States Patent and Trademark Office by Biblica, Inc.™

The Holy Bible, Berean Study Bible, BSB Copyright ©2016 by Bible Hub Used by Permission. All Rights Reserved Worldwide.

WestBow Press books may be ordered through booksellers or by contacting:

WestBow Press
A Division of Thomas Nelson & Zondervan
1663 Liberty Drive
Bloomington, IN 47403
www.westbowpress.com
1 (866) 928-1240

Because of the dynamic nature of the Internet, any web addresses or links contained in this book may have changed since publication and may no longer be valid. The views expressed in this work are solely those of the author and do not necessarily reflect the views of the publisher, and the publisher hereby disclaims any responsibility for them.

Any people depicted in stock imagery provided by Getty Images are models, and such images are being used for illustrative purposes only. Certain stock imagery © Getty Images.

ISBN: 978-1-9736-2697-8 (sc)
ISBN: 978-1-9736-2696-1 (e)

Print information available on the last page.

WestBow Press rev. date: 06/01/2018

CONTENTS

ACKNOWLEDGMENTS

To the four most incredible human beings I've ever encountered in my life: my best friend and unshakeable supportive husband, Jamie—I love you with all my heart, my three amazing and beautiful children, Faith, Shea, and Jesse—You three continue to teach me the beauty and treasure of unconditional love. I love you mostest. (A special thank you to my daughter who gifted us all with her drawings in and through this book.)

To my parents, Roger and Chris Crownover—Thank you for the Godly foundation and infrastructure you have provided and continue to provide for me. The love my heart holds for both of you is immeasurable.

To my mother-n-law, Denise Lee—The prayer warrior of our family. Thank you for wearing out your knees praying for me and our precious family. You are a gift to us all.

To my mentor, Stephanie Tucker—Your patience, guidance and accurate representation of Jesus, during the storm of my life, led me to the One True Savior.

To my home church, Oak Pointe, thank you for spiritually feeding our family the riches of His love.

To the small circle of friends, Teri, Lisa, Emily, Anna, Cindy and Tammy, who devotedly sat around my kitchen table, week after week, helping me process through the many pages of this book—Your time, love and hearts were, and continue to be, invaluable.

To The Center for Christian Counseling Studies School and to each precious student who gave me an opportunity to teach this material during an eight-week course-thank you. I am forever indebted and eternally grateful.

To my three life-long best friends, Sarah, Laura and Lori. Thank you for being my surrogate sisters of life.

And most of all, to the True Author of this book, as well as the love of my life, Jesus Christ. This is all yours. May you do what only You can do.

FOREWORD

I had read hundreds of Christian self-help books by the time I was thirty years of age. Easily over two-hundred. Probably more, I admit hesitantly.

From Boundaries, to The Search for Significance, to Breaking Free, to How People Grow; they all captivated me. Mostly because that which was harmfully parched on the inside was longing for satisfying hydration from the outside. Only problem, there was no outside hydration gratifying, fulfilling, completing, satisfying enough to quench the brittle heart within.

Every well had a floor, and inevitably, I bottomed out each time I felt I found the river of life. Unbeknownst to me, however, the river of life belonged to the One to whom owned a well of water which never ran dry. Which never disappointed. Which never failed. Which never bottomed out. It filled an aching heart. It soothed an open wound. It satisfied an inner longing. It quenched an internal exhaustion.

I still remember a particular phone call, clearly and vividly. It was just days after I had purchased a new, clean, crisp, soft-covered self-help book filled to the rim of providential promises to free me of toxic relationships, binding strong holds, harmful perfectionism, codependent enablement and addiction of others approval.

At least that's what the cover assured.

I opened-up the first page as my eyes overflowed with a disillusioned hope and a deceitful optimism that this was finally *the* book, *the* answer, *the* remedy to that which was dulling the heart and imprisoning the soul.

So, I read the book.

Truthfully, I devoured the book in one seating, binging on every word while actively engaging in the gluttonous pursuit of comfort. The unquenchable pursuit of freedom. The relentless pursuit of purpose. The persistent pursuit of joy. The unattainable pursuit of answers. The wearied pursuit of, oh yes, r e s t.

Maybe, just maybe, I thought, this author here held the key to my happiness. Maybe, just maybe, she held the hope to my despair. Maybe, just maybe, she held the remedy to my inner ache and the answer to my purposelessness.

I was right about one thing, it most certainly was an Author; just not the one who wrote this book. The Author I was unknowingly searching for was in between the crisp pages. In between the straight lines. In between the black letters. And unknowingly, in my own heart, which searched feverishly for what I had simply obtained all along- the Author and Perfector of my faith.

But that seemed too simple, too complex. And somehow the combining forces of both simplicity and complexity drove my idol-worshipping, broken-minded mentality to shrug away truth. Truth that should, could and would have set this captive free.

I had made a habitual pattern of worshiping that which had been created instead of the Creator (Romans 1:25.) Christian self-help books have been designed and written to draw the eyes of the hurting church and a wounded people to seek Gods face for solution. Yet, instead, my confused mind became obsessed with the assurance that the human author held the solution. In many ways, my faulty belief system encouraged me to believe gifting trumped anointing. Status trumped humility. Spot-light trumped His-Light. Applause trumped character. Being known by multitudes trumped being known by One. My entire mindset was discombobulated and I had developed a serious condition of spiritual vertigo. I had lost all divine vision and direction for the one path which would lead me home.

And so, I did what any rational person with this type of skewed mentality would do; I hounded down the authors contact information.

I sought her voice instead of His face.

I remember the call clearly and vividly with this public speaker and multiple book author. We had spoken via email for a couple of days and chose this day, this moment, this time to speak over the phone. My heart raced with both fearful anxiety and desperate hope as my ear listened intensely to each individual ring. My left hand clung tightly to the book she had written; oozing of underlined sentences, stared words, colored hearts, coffee stained pages and tear stained question marks, now littering the previous clean crisp pages.

Eventually the ringing ceased and a friendly voice calmly and politely said "hello?" After a few short moments of small talk, I emptied it all out. Lamenting, complaining, grieving, weeping, blaming, defending, deflecting. All of it purged forth effortlessly and passionately from the volcanic heart within and into her corner of the world.

She waited patiently for the adult temper tantrum to come to a much needed close and gently shared one piece of advice. Three small words that both exhilarated and completely shattered the desperate heart within:

"let-it-go."

"That's it?" I thought. "Let it go? That's all the advice you have for me? Because if I had the ability, the strength, the power, the know-how-to let it all go, wouldn't of I done that a long time ago?" I could barely mutter out the simple words "thank you" through my quivering lips and deeply disappointed heart before abruptly ending our conversation.

I threw the phone onto the freshly cut blades of green grass where I was sitting on a step of the front porch and began sobbing uncontrollably in the palm of my hands. Her professional answer was to let-it-go and I had zero ability to do such a thing. I felt deeply hopeless. Thoughts flooded my mind with being enslaved to these negative emotions indefinitely. Experiencing these shame messages interminably. Battling these strongholds of un-forgiveness continuously.

And yet, it was precisely here, this hitting rock bottom moment, where I knew I had exhausted all human antidotes. Where God penetratingly spoke far into my anguished spirit and whispered if I was *finally* done searching for artificial living water in wells with holes? He boldly, yet sweetly reminded me that He is the Living Water. He is what I am longing for. What I am chasing, searching, thirsting after; *It was Him.*

This defining moment led to a new found investigative work of digging deep into the knowing of Gods character. I soon realized in order to let-go, the big, small and everything in between, I had to have an unshakeable knowing of the One to whom I was handing over that which must be let-go of.

And He did not disappoint.

Although this was not an overnight transfer, His undeserved kindness, His gentle intimacy, His relentless love, His unfathomable grace, His unwavering faithfulness, His unmovable character; it all led my heart, mind and spirit towards freedom. Until, that is, *letting-go* no longer fueled my pursuit. Letting-go soon became a secondary quest and a natural by-product to the One who now sat on the throne of my heart. Fulfilling every need, satisfying every hunger, comforting every loss, medicating every wound, and supplying every want.

It was Him all along.

The letting go? Well, this I know. *There is no letting go unless we embrace, and not run from, the current suffering God is using to refine us.* Unless we trust the One to whom we are handing it over to. Unless we know that what He has in replace of what we're about to lose is, "Exceedingly, abundantly, immeasurably above all that we might ask, think or imagine" (Ephesians 3:20.)

And let me say with all certainty, *it is,* dear one.

INTRODUCTION

Those who plant with tears will harvest with shouts of joy.
Psalm 126:5

So, what happens exactly in between the days, weeks, months and often years of, "Planting with tears and harvesting with shouts of joy," which Psalm 126:5 refers to, on this often bumpy spiritual journey with Jesus?

This is a series of steps in which God revealed during my own tear-planting to joy-harvesting season. This is not, however, a step-by-step process to follow. Rather, a personal spiritual and biblical outline as to the overview of God's ways, God's promises and God's matchless character. Locking our eyes on Him; the Solution, the Answer, the Remedy, the Antidote, the Cure for *all* things broken—and not the steps, will enable us to experience the tender, redeeming, ridiculous, sufficient, transformational, unfathomable love administered and deposited perfectly into the deepest hurting, darkest broken and depleted spaces of the heart.

Over the decade, I've begun to recognize patterns, both

in experience and scripture, of Gods divine order. Taking that which is held captive, God reaches into the secret places of our shame and pours His healing presence into every hidden corner and crevice of their toxic bitter roots. The world promises, "Superficial treatment for our mortal wounds; giving assurance of peace when there is no peace" (Jer. 6:14.) Yet, the only real, authentic, true, genuine, generationally impacting peace comes only from the Author of Peace Himself. There is no other way.

He is it.

Peace, freedom, joy, contentment, rest; they're all experiences our human soul longs to live-in, moment by moment, would you agree? To assuredly walk, in-spite of the grievous circumstances of our everyday life, knowing we are deeply, tenderly, sweetly, fully, undeservingly loved by the One who IS love. Yes, this is indeed where our hearts will be set free from all forms of bondage, joy-deprivation, deceit, fear, shame, guilt, confusion, anger and exhaustion.

There's a season which takes place, agriculturally, in between the sowing and the reaping; which is why there, too, is a season between our current suffering (planting in tears) and obtaining freedom (harvesting joy.) The scars, the suffering, the sorrow; they're the internal earth, the dark fertile grounds of the heart in which God has prepared for the depositing of the deeply anticipated and desperately needed seed of hope. Seedlings containing a new way. A new vision. A new joy. A new identity. A new.

Found only in the dark.

Because it's while in the dark, seeds break open.

Because it's while in the dark, roots emerge.
Because it's while in the dark, miracle of life is formed.

And at the heightened risk of avoiding the dark seasons, the dark circumstances, the dark chapters, the dark days, the dark moments—there'd be no genuinely-authentic, freedom-providing, joy-installing, peace-erecting, life-offering gift of freedom.

With God's unfathomable power, He places His authentic fingerprint on the life-altering ingredients needed to saturate and fill our atmosphere, our lives, our hearts with the precise and perfect nutrients needed to fully grow and develop us into our purpose. A purpose predesigned for our specific and unique and purposeful lives.

My prayer for you, for me, for us all on this Falling North journey, is that we would submit to His gentle and kind ways; allowing Him access and permission to have His way, here and now. Taking a firm grip, one finger at a time, onto His trustworthy and strong right hand as He confidently leads our life into the unknown—the unknown bursting at the seams of purpose, of passion, of joy, of refreshment, of rest, of freedom, of LIFE in abundance.

Father, have Your way!

CHAPTER 1

SUFFERING = OBEDIENCE

"Jesus learned obedience by the things He suffered."
Hebrews 5:8

We had a 90 degree Michigan summer evening dinner on the back porch with the family last night. And just as the thought flooded through my head how perfect this moment, this weather, this meal, this company, this conversation was, my middle child interrupted these thoughts and shared he once heard from a movie that *eating peanut butter filled in the cracks of his heart.*

And so, he ate and ate it every day to fill in the aching cracks of his hurting heart; for year's he innocently disclosed with me. He shared, at first, he thought it worked, only to shockingly and disappointingly realize the peanut butter never reached his little hungry heart.

Because it's the love-deprived cracks in our heart which often drive our decision making, our choices, our thoughts, our feelings; I pondered as his words sat on my heart like a lead brick.

It's the cracks in our heart which fling us into the web of a toxic relationship, or compulsive shopping, or over-eating, or obsessive perfectionism, or substance addiction, or work-a-holism, or addictive porn, or passive-aggressive controlling, or codependency, or stinkin-thinkin; the choice is ours and they are ripe for the picking. But could it be, this crack in our heart, this suffering we're enduring, was inherently sown there by God who desired to be the peanut butter, to be the remedy, to be the glue, to be the stitch which binds the broken heart back together?

Just possibly we've given into the enemy's lie and believed counterfeit peanut butter could fill in the cracks, all the while having direct access to the Only One who can sufficiently make us whole, set us free, heal our brokenness, eradicate our soul sickness and release the negative strongholds.

I also wonder had my boy never experienced a crack-in-the-heart (the suffering) would he of been on a quest for a sticky substance to put his heart back together? Could it be that this inherent need, this continual desire to be whole, to be known, to be loved, to be accepted, to be identified, is a gift from God, provided to us by means of suffering?

It's His fingerprint on our hearts saying, *"Seek me and I will be the only and final peanut butter you will ever need."* As my dinner grew increasingly cold and my thoughts increasingly in number, my son's raspy pre-teen voice abruptly cut into the pondering, *"But a couple years ago, mom, Jesus told me He was my peanut butter."*

And there we have it.

As he went back to eating his dinner with a content and satisfied smile across his freckled face, it was in this moment I recognized it was *because* of my son's suffering, and not in-spite of, which lead him to the stillness of obedience in Christ. Which, ultimately, revealed the true Peanut Butter of his heart. Yet, it's this very initial "step" in this Falling North journey which is by far the most difficult one of them all. In fact, regrettably, most never make it past the first milestone of obtaining the True Peanut Butter of their soul.

Why?

Well, first, it's here we find the strongholds of our lives continually yanking us back into the prison of our hearts. This prison being defined as anything, anyone or anyplace, besides Christ Himself, which has power over us. Anything which has enslaved us, captivated us, bonded us into its grip where we have lost *all* ability to say no. To stop. To resist. To break free.

Whether it's more the obvious issues of addictions, relational toxic patterns, habits and/or hang ups-or the hidden issues lying just beneath the radar of control, fear, manipulation, self-loathing, people-pleasing, jealousy, un-forgiveness, depression, anger, resentment, worthlessness, hopelessness, shame, guilt, bitterness; they each have the potential of tormenting the soul while the glimpse of ultimate freedom lurks just outside the prison bars of the heart. And yet, unbeknownst to us, we are shamefully unable to confidently walk out of the prison's wide open door into the unknown and beautiful world of freedom.

I lived most my Christian life in this prison. Longing to

be free from both the obvious and not-so-obvious hidden strongholds of my life. I would set my weary feet towards the open door, often cautiously taking a step or two outside onto the luscious green grass of the winds of freedom, only to run my fearful and shame-based heart back into the cold prison, back to the dysfunctional peanut butter, back to where it was deceitfully safe and dangerously comfortable. Clinging to that which I was not willing to let go.

Last Christmas season, my youngest uninhibitedly sang Christmas carols, with a bell draped around his neck, as we drove home from school this particular cold and wintery afternoon.

He smiled with his sweet, gentle and amused eyes as he shared with me the traditional story behind the bell around his neck. "Mrs. Pearson gave me this, Mom," he said with great enthusiasm, as he proceeded to ring it harder just in case I hadn't heard it the countless times before.

I was sweetly amused at the simple joy he was experiencing with this gold bell. A bell, which in return, brought him spontaneous laughter. Unreserved happiness. Innocent pleasure. But strangely for a moment, as if turning mute on the sound system to life, the car fell silent. The singing, the ringing, the sounds of Christmas came to an abrupt pause as he intensively white knuckled the bell in the right palm of his ten-year old hand. Still shaking the bell with great vigor and passion, the sound of the bell fell completely mute. Silent. And that's precisely when he cut through the unexpected and awkward silence, and said it.

The secret to life, that is.

"Mom," he insightfully shared, "If I hold on too tight to this bell, it doesn't ring. I need to let go for it to fulfill its purpose." Every letter of those few wise words spoken through this child seemed to linger in the now luke warm air of the car. As Jesse released the bell from the grips of his little hand, he gently let-go, one finger at a time, and delightfully continued to ring the bell.

Let go, huh.

It's in the letting-go we find purpose, isn't it? We find identity. We find meaning. We find freedom. We find life. The purpose of that small and simple Christmas bell draped around the soft skin of his neck was to bring joy to a child's heart. Yet when clung too tight, its sole purpose was obsolete.

And how human nature is still strangely drawn and naively tempted to cling. To cling too tight to him or her. To cling too tight to past mistakes, to regret, to shame, to unforgiveness, to assumptions, to guilt, to idols, to control, to finances, to insecurities, to pride, to resentments, to hatred, to lies.

To cling.

Because it's in the whom I'm clinging to during times of insecurity is where I'll find my security. And how often I ashamedly find my white knuckled grip wrapped around too tightly a false security. A delusional hope. A fabricated happiness. A counterfeit truth.

All the while, shaking the bell of life with passionate vigor and relentless zeal, yet not fulfilling God's hand knit purpose and calling; simply due to the destructive clinging diminishing the ringing. I suppose that's why Jesus Himself said, "If you cling to your life, you will lose it. And if you let-it-go, you will find it" (Matthew 10:39.)

As the author of life, Jesus has given invaluable direction for the meaning of life; letting-go so that He Alone can fulfill and expose the very purpose hand designed for each and every life. A life which supersedes that of the greatest imagination. And yet, letting go is no simple feat. No indeed.

It wasn't until I was broken open did I come to a place of desiring that which I was unaware was in the waiting room of life. Once the fingers were willing to be released, one by one, of my white knuckled clenched grip, could I experience the unimaginable gift of purpose. Which, in return, ushered in the very presence of rest. A rest where exhaustion and heavy negative emotions were no longer dictating that of my reality, but rather surrender, reverence, trust and an unfathomable experience of the love of God, formed the way I now operated and shaped my life.

I have found it to be undoubtedly true that Jesus is indeed the cure for the insecure. And the more I let-go of that which depletes me of the very purpose of my existence, the more I find my life.

And so, here we are desiring to make a change, longing to obtain rest, thirsty for freedom, parched for joy, hungry for restoration, desperate to trust-and yet chained and enslaved to that which has control and power over our ability to fully offer God our entire self.

Take note right here sweet one, God is after your heart. Always the heart.

God does not desire for us to stay here for one. more. minute. Every millisecond our feet stay flat inside these prison floors, licking our lips of fraudulent peanut butter, His heart is breaking. And yet, in His unfathomable goodness, He knows it's these very familiar, ugly, rotting, closing-in prison walls which will ultimately lead us into His safe, unfailing, restful and life-giving arms (Acts 5:18-20.)

At a point of experiencing my own internal prison, I wrote out these very words to God. With tears dropping one by one down my flush cheeks and into God's collection of His no-tear-wasted vile, I wrote this letter out of pure desperation and exhaustion during a hopeless and desperate season of marital turmoil. Maybe you're in a similar season, or quite possibly something all together different. But whatever the season you may be experiencing, my prayer is that these words inspire, encourage and lead your heart to the One & Only Remedy.

God,

If one more person tells me to trust You.... I simply don't know if I'll survive it. Better yet, if they'll survive it. Because the truth is, when they offer me this piece of well-meaning advice, it feels like salt being smothered and smeared directly into my raw and bloody and open wound.

A wound infested infected inflamed with this gripping dark shame covering the internal pain of my heart.

And as much as I know their advice comes from a good place—from a rightful truthful helpful place desiring to steer my pain, my fear, my confusion, my heartache, my loss towards a destination of rest; asking me to do the impossible right now, in this here storm, is stacking further lead bricks of shame onto the already multiple existing ones.

So many bricks.

Their advice is reminding me it's simply just one more thing, amongst the numerous other ones, of that which I'm incapable of doing— trusting You.

Asking me to trust You is causing more shame. Further pain. Deeper infection.

Because, how do I trust You when trusting others has proven to be unsafe? How do I trust You when it looks like You've permitted this heartache?

How do I trust You when I don't believe You could possibly still love me with all the wrong choices I've made?

How do I trust You when I don't even know if You're actually trustworthy?

Asking me to trust You while in the typhoon of my life is causing me to sink further down into the pit of despair. And I'm sinking Lord.

But I hold to one piece of advice that one friend gave me. You know the one. The precious friend who oozed of inexplainable peace and radiated an inexplicable love. She didn't tell me to trust You.

She didn't tell me to let-go & let-God. No, Your daughter told me that Your love for me was beyond my limited comprehension. It was beyond my greatest imagination. It was beyond my deepest understanding.

She told me that You're a God who leaves the 99 to find me.

To search for me.

To rescue me.

To restore me.

To love me.

She told me You hear & rescue me when I call to You for help (Psalm 34.17.) She told me You're close to the broken hearted and rescue those whose spirits are crushed (Psalm 34.18.)

She told me You don't ignore the cries of those who suffer (Psalm 9.12.) She told me You're a shelter for those who are weighed down with burden, pain, hurts, grief and loss (Psalm 91.2.) She told me You're a refuge in times of trouble (Psalm 9.9.) She told me You heal the broken hearted and bind up my wounds (Psalm 147.3.) She told me that You **are** love and You loved me first (1 John 4.16.)

Come to think of it, she never did mention to trust You, God. It's quite possible she knew trusting You is impossible without first knowing Your incomprehensible, unimaginable, undeserving love for me, **first.**

In spite of what I've done, or haven't done.

In spite of what I've thought, or haven't thought.

In spite of what I've said, or haven't said.

In spite of how un-loveable I actually feel.

She knew the secret component needed <u>first</u> in order to trust You, God- a **knowing of Your love for me.** *It must start there.*

And, I have this beautiful hunch God, it also ends there.

As I close this letter, Father, I'm hearing You gently whisper into the wounded places of the heart, "You don't have to trust me just yet, my child. But know this... My love for you was first, is first, and will always be first. If you allow your heart to receive that which is undeserved, you will organically sense the life-altering, life-giving, natural-byproduct of a trust in the One who's always worth trusting. Because My love for you, even in your worst, is enough."

I love you, too, God
Joyelle

In the book of Zechariah, a young prophet born into Babylonian captivity, shared and confirmed with us God's design and purpose for suffering. Zachariah 13:9 states, *"I will bring that group through the fire (suffering) and make them pure. I will refine them like silver and purify them like gold. They will call on my name and I will answer them. I will say, 'These are my people,' and they will say, 'The Lord is our God.' "*

God makes it clear we *must* go through fire to be:
*Purified like gold.
*Refined like silver.

And then, and only then:
1. I will call on His name.
2. He will answer me.
3. He will say "This is my child."
4. I will say "The Lord is my God."

We see clearly and vividly in this simple passage that our suffering, our purification, our refinement, our pruning is the very doorway needed to propel us into a deeper, higher, longer, wider, passionate, life-altering relationship with the Lover and Guardian of our soul (1 Peter 2:25.)

And yet we may find ourselves circling around the same mountain over and over again, until one day we recognize we are living out the very definition of insanity. Yet it's here in the web of this insanity, this exhaustion, this frustration— *this suffering,* which has undoubtedly lead us to obedience; for we've exhausted all other options. The suffering in which God uses to catapult us into the safe-haven of sweet obedience, is the kind which will enable us to finally and ultimately say, "Okay, God, I'll do it Your way. I can't live like this, or endure this pain, or smell the prison stench for one more moment. Have Your way" (Psalm 131:2.)

I remember vividly giving birth to each of my three little ones. And while at first I used careful discretion with the hospital staff and visitors by covering up when possible, all too soon, as the contraction pain in-creased, my shame ultimately de-creased. At the highest level of excruciating pain, I wasn't the least interested &/or bothered in who was witnessing my vulnerability and my fully exposed baby mama body. I simply wanted the pain to cease. And that's why, dear friend, it's in this precise moment, in this precise place, in this precise position, *the pain will have finally outweighed the shame.* Because we can't heal until we reveal. And we can't reveal until we feel. And we can't feel until we kneel.

And, as a result of these most beautiful pain-increased, shame-decreased situations, He stills our restless soul. He pauses our idol-worshipping heart. He shelves our counterfeit comforts. And, simultaneously, cautiously steps our weary and wounded heart out the doorway of the prison walls within, gently leading us to the only Peanut Butter we will *ever* need.

This timid, fearful, yet courageous footstep toward the beauty of obedience, of letting-it-go, of surrender-begins with suffering. Yet even though God, in His immeasurable kindness, forewarns us in His life-supplying, life-giving, life-altering Word that this suffering will be inevitable, unavoidable and inescapable, take heart dear friend, because this we know-- **It will never be wasted (Romans 8:28.)**

Your obedience will lead to your deliverance.
(Luke 17:14.)

"Great moves of God are preceded by great acts of obedience."
-Steven Furtick

Thought to ponder:

Obedience/sacrifice, mentioned here in Chapter one, doesn't require heart transformation. It's strictly behavior modification at this point. Which is why this is indeed the most difficult transition of them all. Romans 2:29 tells us, "A person with a changed heart seeks praise from God, not people." This initial step of obedience/sacrifice will still have a heart condition choosing to please people instead of God. However, as the next steps begin to be organically experienced, soon the desire to please will turn from people to God as we move beyond "obedience" and into a beautiful thing called "surrender."

For example, when suffering has led to obedience (first phase) it's simply a willful act fueled from a continual suffering that we want-no-more. At this point, it's probably safe to say our pain has finally outweighed our shame, and we reluctantly, yet resolvedly, place down the peanut butter jar of the heart and choose to do it God's way.

However, when surrender has taken place, we submit as a natural byproduct of a heart transformation and an internal anchored love of Christ within the deepest reservoir of our soul. Surrender proves our commitment, our devotion, our love towards Him (John 14:23.) and is exhibited as a pure, genuine, holy response of His love for us. Whereas obedience/sacrifice is done out of exhaustion and desperation from a way of life which simply was not working.

Questions to ponder w/ God

1. What is your peanut butter today? The one thing, person, place, desire in which God has consistently whispered in your heart it's time to lay down (obedience)?

2. Write out the fears attached to releasing these counterfeit comforts, idols, habits, addictions, strongholds, etc.

3. Write out a prayer asking God to take it from you, as He gently places your hand into his and walks you out of the prison doors, into your true-identity.

Scriptures

<u>Romans 5:3-5</u>

<u>2 Corinthians 4:17</u>

<u>1 Peter 4:1-2</u>

<u>1 Peter 3:14</u>

<u>Psalm 94:12-13</u>

Joyelle Lee

<u>Philippians 1:29</u>

<u>Philippians 3:10</u>

<u>Matthew 10:38-39</u>

<u>Deuteronomy 8:3</u>

<u>1 Peter 2:21</u>

<u>psalm 71:20</u>

Drawing Closer

1. Begin writing out your story, asking the Holy Spirit to reveal memories, moments, events, traumas, joys-and everything in between. Jesus IS light and desires to light up every dark, hidden, secret corner of the heart. Shame instantaneously dissolves in light. It can not grow, produce or continue to thrive in the presence of light. Expose anything and everything hidden, knowing we can't heal unless we feel.

2. Begin reading His word daily. Purchase a bible in which the translation matches your heart. I prefer an NLT due to its accurate simplicity. However, there are many other translations. Just as we plug in our phones each evening and enjoy fresh cold milk from our plugged-in fridge, we also must plug-into the Only sufficient energy source for the heart, mind and soul. This isn't a legalistic mentality, but a heart-recognition that the parched soul within needs tending to. It's here we place our ears on the chest of our Father and receive His life-giving words and His perfect peace, each and every day, so that we can move and operate no longer on empty, but from an overflow of His perfect power and love. It's been said that an unexamined life isn't worth living. Allow God to examine your heart each day so that He can reveal the purpose and plan He has pre-established on your life; and the make-no-sense depth of love He has for you.

3. Journal. Yes, more writing, but this tool is a game changer. I've been journaling for years and recognize

I am nothing to anyone if I am not first infused and overflowing of the love of Jesus. Before anyone else, before any phone call, any text, any email, any distraction—we need to reveal every corner of the heart before the One who is Light. It's here in the intimacy of our transparency, we can safely share that which we normally would repress and stuff. Where we can tell on those who need to be told on. Where we can weep over that which has caused sorrow. Where we can rejoice in the joy and goodness of God. Where we can shed our mask and reveal our authentic fragile self without the fear of rejection. It's here, with our pen in hand and an open slate, where we will see God with our own eyes (Job 42:5.)

What You're saying to me, God....

_____

_____

_____

_____

_____

_____

_____

_____

_____

_____

_____

_____

_____

_____

_____

_____

My prayer to You, Father....

_____

_____

_____

_____

_____

_____

_____

_____

_____

_____

_____

_____

_____

_____

NOTHING

IS

wasted

CHAPTER 2

OBEDIENCE = EXPERIENCING HIS LOVE

*"But for those who obey God's word truly
show how completely they love Him. That
is how we know we are living in Him."*
1 John 2:5

Sometimes it still overwhelms me having two seventeen-inch titanium bars running up and down my spine in order to keep it straight.

A spine which was prone to wander, to curve beyond its boundaries, to engage in that which was beyond its God-given design. It's no wonder God uses analogies such as *straight* paths, *straight* ways, *straight* roads, *straight* feet and *straight* direction when describing a life of obedience which ultimately leads to a life experiencing His redeeming, life-altering, life-supplying love.

God's in the business of restoring the crooked spinal

column of the heart and finds deep satisfaction in being the surgeon to our life. Taking our curved, wandering, self-destructive heart and implanting His divine, supernatural, life giving guard rails along the prone-to-wander soul--straightening the very central support beam of our life so that our wandering, curving, crooked heart would stay where it's safe. Where it's protected. Where it's offering life to others. Where it's experiencing God's love. Where it's bearing generational changing fruit. Where it's tasting sweetness of hope. Where it's a constant flow of blessing and no longer a generational destructive curse.

It was in the curved path of both my life and spine where pain and suffering were experienced. Where conflict of purpose was tasted. Where confusion of boundaries was cultivated. Since the curve of my spine resisted staying within its safe boundaries of protection, the body, the organs, the brain, the nerves were all negatively influenced by the health of the spine. And how often, I too, see how my children, my husband, my friends, my family, my community are all affected by the condition and health of the spine of my heart. A crooked heart has enough power to set a life off balance and keep us actively searching for the next counterfeit peanut butter jar.

Jeremiah 50:5 says, "They will start *back home* again. They will **bind** themselves to the Lord with an eternal covenant that'll never be forgotten." After much *suffering*, chronic pain, daily exhaustion, consuming fear, anxious thoughts, restless sleeps, toxic thinking, I too, started home again towards obedience. And at the moment I started my journey back home, God bound the vertebrates of my heart to His perfect, redeeming, restful, joy-filled titanium bars of His unfailing love. Bars which took the heart's curved path, and by the steady hands of the Great Physician, surgically straightened it with the active ingredient of His love. Releasing me of the shame which gripped my thought's, the fear which consumed my mind, the fictitious love which deceived the heart and the curve which disfigured the soul.

God interjects His ingredient of pure love into our own feeble human heart, enabling a season of growth, of self-evaluation, of healing, of *receiving the experience of His divine love*. It's here which He's given access to straighten out the curves, level out the mountains, raise up the valleys, smooth out the path (Isaiah 40:3-5) and place His titanium guard rails along the boundary of the crooked heart. As a result we are protected, guided, mentored, nurtured, re-parented and filled with a continual flowing gush of Jesus' enough love.

If you have found yourself on the crooked path of life, there is no question as to why you are reading this. He has brought you here, in this place, at this time, so that He alone can surgically transfer your heart into a straight, smooth and guard-railed path of obedience. A path offering the deeply rooted experience of His love, the anchored grip of His hope, the steadfast assurance of His rest, the life-supplying gift of His joy and the generational providing antidote of His freedom.

It was straight out of college where I worked at an orphanage with young girls between the ages of four and eleven. Precious young ones who no doubt taught me significantly more than I could have taught them. And yet, it was here, in this orphanage where I was given the opportunity and the privilege of being placed in a position to better comprehend the deeper driving components fueling the orphan mentality.

Since I worked the 3:pm to midnight shift, the opportunity to do life with them in a more intimate, personal and nurturing environment was given to me. Homework, dinner, psychological processing, bedtime tuck-ins; these were each part of my every day routine with the girls. Yet, just about every day I came into work, the day shift would share one of our girls had run away that particular morning. And, as it never failed, I'd tuck this sweet one into bed the following evening after she had been safely located, and looked far into her lost and deeply saddened eyes, saying, "Where were you running to? What were you running towards?"

And without the slightest of hesitation or differentiation of reasons, she'd look up at me and share, "Nowhere. I was just running away from here." You see, it wasn't the orphanage these loved ones were running from. They were running from the tormenting emptiness of their heart. They were running from the haunting breach in their foundation. They were running from the love deprivation of their soul. They were running from the relentless ghost of constant fear.

They were running, and running fast in the wrong direction. And when our orphan mentality, fueled by a deep love-deprivation, is offered the choice between fight or flight, flight is instinctively chosen, hands down, every time. Because what we often don't realize is that wherever, whenever and to whomever we run, the ghosts will always follow.

An orphan mentality fuels the individual to lie, to manipulate, to fear, to run, to defend, to stuff, to deflect, to self-destruct; simply because the very ones who were supposed to supply the all-sufficient love, to administer the gentle comfort, to confidently guide the way, to sweetly nurture the pain, to compassionately heal the wounds-were non-existent. Forced into survival mode, the orphan's internal resources and limited energy were used solely on themselves, just to make it through another day.

And what society might label a narcissist personality, an internally dangerous anger, a chronic liar, a manipulative disposition, an anxious complexion-may simply be a case of an orphan mentality. A mentality where we truly don't know the love of our Father, and as a direct by-product, we don't know to whom we belong. We don't know who we are.

Because a lack of love is an identity issue. And a lack of identity is a love issue.

In Matthew 3.16, Jesus is baptized by John the Baptist. Immediately after He is lifted from the water and, "The heavens opened and He saw the Spirit of God descending like a dove and settling on Him. And a voice from heaven said, 'This is my dearly loved son, who brings me great joy.'"

After Jesus received the Holy Spirit, God shared three distinct truths:

1. He is loved.
2. He is God's son.
3. He brings God great joy.

These three truths are also our truths today.

Romans 5:5 confirms this life-altering reality by reminding us that it's the Holy Spirit who administers God's love deep into the core of our belief system. And, in conjunction, Romans 8:16 confirms to what Matthew revealed through the baptism of Jesus—when, "His Spirit co-joins with our spirit, it is affirmed and accomplished that we are indeed His adopted child in whom He is well pleased and brought much joy" (which we'll discuss in greater detail in chapter 7.)

Ironically, the more I loved on these precious girls in the orphanage, the more they resisted, redirected, rejected that which my heart desired to give them. They didn't fully trust the love I desired to share, simply because they had never been offered it, especially during the window their parched souls required it the most. How often we, as adopted children and heirs of God, consciously and often unconsciously lack the unshakeable trust in His unfailing love, simply because of the insufficient, inaccurate, unavailable, skewed, broken, dysfunctional love of another human being.

In Luke 6:27, Jesus gives us a sneak preview as to what a daughter, a son, a child adopted by their Maker and loved well by their Father exemplifies, naturally, as a result of knowing, receiving, embracing, participating, accepting and experiencing their Daddy's perfect love. Our acknowledgment, our reception, our knowing, our experience of our Father's love will position the former-orphan heart to:

1. Love our enemies.
2. Do good to those who hate us.
3. Bless those who curse us.
4. Offer the other cheek to be slapped.
5. Offer our shirt when our coat has been taken.
6. Give to those in need who ask.
7. Don't try to get back that which was taken away.
8. Do to others as we'd like them to do to us.

*Luke 6:27-31

And yet, how often we respond to life as an orphan, unable to live out this type of unfailing love. This type of radical selflessness. This type of unconditional grace. This type of immeasurable kindness.

Because, we can't give what we don't have.

Our Father, at this very moment, is oozing of excitement to hand deliver you, His precious and loved child, the kind of wondrous life, the kind of perplexing love, the kind of unthinkable hope, the kind of unspeakable joy our inner spirit was delicately crafted and purposefully positioned to receive.

Yet, instead, we often give into the enemy's crafty tactics and fear the unknown-hanging out in survival mode while the truth of being adopted and loved perfectly and completely and sufficiently and fully by our good Father hides under the weight of our former shame, guilt, fear and emotional malnourishment. Yet, it's the One who holds the purest, deepest, most penetrating love imaginable who also has cupboards overflowing of the richest, satisfying and nourishing ingredients necessary to saturate *every* need, *every* hurt, *every* violation, *every* pain (Romans 8:15-17.)

And so, here we are, staring eyeball to eyeball with the obvious relentless question of the heart. How do we take this theological head knowledge of the immensity, the sufficiency, the enough-ness of His love, down the eighteen-inch journey to the orphan heart—a heart which sincerely desires to believe, receive and conceive this truth? It's simply found within the *stillness* of our obedience (Psalm 46:10.)

From obedience to experiencing His love, a divine intimate, natural, powerful transfer of our sufferings into His perfect loving hands of a gentle Father, enables the soul to *experience* an intimate love which supersedes not only expectations, but all understanding; while fully saturating the crumbling spaces of our former hungry and parched heart (Ephesians 3:19.)

But this I know, from all too personal of an experience, when we release that which we know must be sacrificed in order to move forward in freedom, we may experience an unusual amount of vulnerability, of loneliness and of fear. The deep pain we've repressed from our past, or the wounds we've artificially medicated, or the lies we've lived out as truth—the heart will feel foreign and uncomfortable without them; *temporarily, that is*. And yet, it's these difficult and heart-wrenching emotions which are the *very* elements God will use to radiate the power of His all-encompassing love straight into our hurting, wounded and divided heart. It's here where you, my dear friend, will finally fully, completely, beautifully and wonderfully receive your Papa's love- a love which has been infused in your heart from the moment of your existence.

Because when, who or what we may have run to during times of insecurity is no longer an option, we will begin to experience the unshakeable security, the matchless refuge, the indisputable safe-haven of Jesus Christ (Psalm 144:2.) While formerly chasing and fixing our eyes on our prior counterfeit comforts, we were unable to fully experience the depth of His security and the immensity of His love-simply because we turned to someone or something else during those times of paralyzing insecurity.

Yet, it's in this particular phase of <u>Obedience = Experiencing His Love</u>, where the sweetest and most beautiful transition will manifest itself above all the other phases ahead of us in the chapters to come. Because It's here where love becomes the cure for the insecure, and our new found security, in His arms, becomes the anchor to the soul (Hebrews 6:19.)

It will also become the greatest significance and feat of our life, day by day, to keep the flow of the Holy Spirit rushing to and fro, within the confinement of our heart. Refusing to allow anything or anyone to quench or stifle His presence, *God's love* (Romans 5:5) and our *adoption status* (Romans 8:16) will continue to operate as the two sole necessary and essential ingredients— ingredient's needed to position the former orphan heart to sit confidently in the fertile soil of His unending, unlimited, bottomless, reservoir of love.

And so, loved one, before moving onto the next "phase," camp out here. Stay awhile. Allow Christ to speak into the dark corners of your heart so that He can fully transfer your new obedience into first-hand experience of an all sufficient Love which *will* enable you to never go back.

"Define yourself as one radically loved by God. This is your true self. Every other identity is an illusion."
–Brennan Manning

31

Questions to ponder w/ God

1. Do you find yourself operating from an orphan mentality instead of the adopted daughter that you are? If so, how and why?

2. What is it you're still holding onto that is prohibiting you from fully experiencing your Father's perfect love? List all the areas below along with the 'fear' attached to each one.

3. If you are beginning to experience His love in this phase, how is this impacting your everyday life?

Scriptures

1 John 4:18

John 4:34

1 John 2:5

John 14:23-24

Romans 5:5

Joyelle Lee

<u>Romans 8:15-17</u>

<u>Deuteronomy 7:9</u>

<u>Zephaniah 3:17</u>

<u>Psalm 119:75-76</u>

<u>Psalm 91:14</u>

What You're saying to me, God....

_____

_____

_____

_____

_____

_____

_____

_____

_____

_____

_____

_____

_____

_____

_____

My prayer to You, Father....

_____

_____

_____

_____

_____

_____

_____

_____

_____

_____

_____

_____

_____

_____

I seek you

CHAPTER 3

EXPERIENCING HIS LOVE = REVERENCE

"...When they heard that the Lord was concerned about them and had seen their misery, they bowed down and worshiped."
Exodus 4:31

I was twenty years old when approached by a man in the back cassette-tape isle of the Borders Bookstore music department. A stranger with smooth words oozing easily and carelessly from his mouth, slowly jamming into one another while entering my ears like a noisy gong alarming me to run. Flee. Search aggressively for the nearest exit. Yet my body was entirely motionless and strangely paralyzed. Unable to speak or move past the chaotic and abrasive noise flowing from his misleading lips and soon his twisted and deceptive hands, he chose to invade personal boundaries without so much an inkling of an invitation to that which he desired to see, touch, feel.

It's now been twenty-two years since that spring Saturday afternoon, and yet I still hear the dark echo of his voice. I still know the distinct smell of the plastic wrapped cassette-tapes lined up alphabetically in the shelves surrounding him. I still see the outline of his twisted smile, his wandering hands, his overpowering stature, his deceptive shiny words. Yup, It's all still there. But, it was this one unforeseen moment in time which had enough power, enough influence, enough puncture to taint my view on God.

One moment.

Satan's greatest tactic is to enable men, people, strangers, pastors, friends, family, authority figures to misuse their position so that we believe a twisted version of who and what love represents, therefore tainting the correct depiction of who God ultimately is. And often, subconsciously, we have difficulty differentiating the two.

If the enemy can tempt us to mistrust the transforming promises, the steadfast character, the unfathomable love and the unconditional faithfulness of God, then he has succeeded in his fulltime mission. A mission twisted and deceptive enough to keep us from experiencing the rejuvenating power of God's love which ultimately blocks our heart from encountering a deep, life-impacting, heart-transforming reverence for Jesus.

It's possible your experience wasn't with a stranger, but with someone who was supposed to care for you, shepherd you, love you, protect you. Instead, they took advantage of you, left you, deceived you, wounded you. Quite possibly, without even your knowing, your relationship with God has been tainted by someone else's poor choice, an unmet need, or simply the failure of another's role. And, as a result, instead of safety, God began to slowly represent uncertainty. Instead of kindness, judgement. Instead of patience, anger. Instead of stability, insecurity. Instead of trust, doubt. Instead of faithfulness, disloyalty. Instead of comfort, fear. Instead of forgiveness, condemnation. Instead of reverence, suspicion. All of which often reside in the deepest reservoir of the belief system of an individual who's been injured, rejected, violated or wounded physically, mentally, emotionally and/ or spiritually at the hands of another.

There's no doubt the enemy sought to taint my perception of God that day. And, if I'm completely honest with myself, I'm slowly recognizing how this experience, hand crafted by satan himself, was faintly woven into my every day interactions in both my awareness of God's personal love and my ability to fully revere Him. Yet, it was precisely here where God took the heaps of shame polluting my heart and plowed up the soil within.

Jeremiah 4:3 says that God plows up the hard ground of the heart. It's in this plowing process which involves taking the decomposition within and tilting it until it turns into fresh, pure and fertile soil. God takes our unmet needs, our confusion, our pain, our violations- the garbage and decomposition of our circumstances and plows the heart until the remnants of the enemy's ashes turn into good, beautiful, fertile soil. God doesn't always choose to eradicate, but to recreate; producing within us a deep abiding, awe-inspiring reverence for a God who brings the dead back to life and who creates new things out of nothing" (Romans 4:17.)

And so, for every person who's familiar with my experience, or quite possibly far worse, I *need* you to hear this; God's not that guy. Not that woman. Not that unavailable earthly parent. The one who left you. Who betrayed you. Who violated you. Who rejected you. Who deceived you. Who didn't notice you. Who looked down on you. Who disappointed you. Who lied to you. Who shamed you. No, precious one, God is not that person. In fact, it goes against every fiber of His character to be anything *but* perfect.

Webster defines perfection as, "The condition, state, or quality of being free or as free as possible from all flaws or defects." God is not only perfect, but supersedes even the limitations of perfection. "Even perfection has its limits, but your commands have **no limit**" (Psalm 119:96.) God Alone is the Perfect Father, the Faithful Husband, the Wise Counselor, the Strong Protector, the Matchless Healer, the Tender Comforter, the Fierce Leader, the Constant Companion, the Great Physician, the Revealer of Mysteries, the Living Water, the Prince of Peace, the Life Giving Light. And, as John 21:25 reminds us, "If they were all written down I suppose that even the whole world would not have the room for the book that would be written." This truth, in and of itself, naturally places our spirit in a humble, submissive, safe position of reverence before a God who exceeds even our greatest expectations and satisfies *every* need (Acts 17:25.)

Our finite minds cannot begin to fully understand the depths, the heights, the lengths, the widths of His deeply intimate, uniquely personal and undiluted purified love (Ephesians 3:18.) A love which drives our hearts into a complete expression of a fall-to-your-knees reverence for a God who finds us radiantly beautiful, perfectly made and inherently precious; based simply on *nothing* we have thought, said or done. *Nothing* can shift His unreserved, unconditional, immeasurable, immovable, no-strings attached love towards you, towards me, towards us.

"...<u>Nothing</u> can ever separate me from the love of God. Neither death or life, neither angels or demons, neither my fears for today or my worries for tomorrow- not even the powers of hell can separate me from the Love of God. No power in the sky above or in the earth below- indeed, <u>nothing</u> in all creation will ever be able to separate us from the love of God that is revealed in Christ Jesus our Lord" (Romans 8:38.)

God repeatedly reminds us that He *delights* in showing His unfailing love (Micah 7:18.) A love where unadulterated faithfulness and transforming perfection collide into the hungry heart with faultless unity. It's here He takes that which the enemy sowed for destruction and plows up the pride, the anger, the pain, the shame, the hurt, the unmet needs-- and cultivates a harvest of tender humility and an unshakeable reverence to the One who gently whispers in the ear, *"Come to me, all who are weary and burdened, and I will give you rest"* (Matthew 11:28 NIV.) *"I have loved you with an everlasting love. With unfailing love, I have drawn you to Myself"* (Jeremiah 31:3.)

As we learned in the last chapter, we simply can't give what we don't currently have. And, if we've never permitted God's unfailing love access and reign in the deepest reservoir of the heart, it will be near impossible for us to love Him wholeheartedly in return. We love God because He first loved us. (1 John 4:19.) Reverence unlocks love, freeing the shackled heart to experience not only His liberating love, but the redemptive experience of loving Him in return. It's the kind of pure, holy, good, perfect, pleasing, restoring love which He first gave us. And, as a result, we now have both the desire and the ability to give from that which we have been given-- a love by the One who *is* love (1 John 4:8.)

"Love God with all your heart, with all your soul and with all your mind. This is the first and greatest commandment. A second is equally important; Love your neighbor as yourself. The entire law and all the demands of the prophets are based on these two commandments" (Matthew 22:37-40.)

Jesus shares these two life-giving instructions which insure a life of internal joy, of righteous fruit, of super natural power, of matchless wisdom, of agape love, of deep knowledge, of fulfilling purpose, of divine holiness and of eternal rest. Just two life-supplying directions which sum up the entirety of His Word and enable us to avoid, "Unbearable religious demands" (Luke 11:46) while sufficiently providing us with promises of life and peace, in abundance. These are the most powerful, active and alive instructions ever given to mankind. *The secret to life.* And yet, these promises can only be fulfilled and accomplished by *receiving* and accepting His love first. Without receiving from Him, every relational area in our life will be affected-giving to and loving others through an exhausted supply of limited love (Ephesians 5:21.)

Isaiah 33:6 says, "The fear of the Lord will be your treasure." Isaiah 45:3 also further shares that, "He will give you treasures hidden in the darkness- secret riches." If reverence, as stated in Isaiah 33:6 is our ultimate and most satisfying treasure in life, then Isaiah 45:3 says that this particular treasure can *only* be found in the dark. In the dark seasons. In the dark circumstances. In the dark emotions. In the dark. Isaiah 45:3 also says, "I will do this (providing treasures in the dark) so you may know that I am the Lord, the God of Israel, the One who calls you by name."

He knows you by name, dear one. The same God, who in Isaiah 40:12-15 says, *"Who else has held the oceans in His hand? Who else has measured off the heavens with His fingers? Who else knows the weight of the earth or has weighed the mountains and hills on the scale? Who is able to advise the Spirit of the Lord? Who knows enough to give Him advice or teach Him? Has the Lord ever needed anyone's advice? Does He need instruction about what is good? Did someone teach Him what is right or show Him the path of justice? No, for all the nations of the world are but a drop in the bucket. They are nothing more than dust on the scales. He picks up the whole earth as though it were a grain of sand."*

Yes, this same God, the One who picks up the whole earth as though it were a tiny grain of sand, knows *your* name. Because, He's also the same God who carried you before you were born (Isaiah 46:3) and promises to, *"Be your God throughout your lifetime, until your hair is white with age. "I made you, and I will care for you. I will carry you along and save you."'* It's in this transformative revelation where the treasure of our heart will recognize reverence and intimacy are not separate entities, but synchronized resources from the very hand of a God who's both incomprehensibly enormous and unfathomably intimate.

There's rest in the ingredient of reverence, as noted by Christ Himself. "Then Jesus said, "Come to me all of you

who are weary and carry heavy burdens, and I will give you rest. Take my yoke upon you. Let me teach you, because I am humble and gentle at heart, and you will find rest for your souls. For my yoke is easy to bear and the burden is light'" (Matthew 11:28-30.)
Most assuredly, rest is found here.

Yet, how often we believe the strenuous and burdensome lie that finding the internal negative root (the *reason* for our current emotional pain) is solely our job to locate. To eradicate. To castrate. However, hold this truth tightly in the core of your belief system-it's God who's commissioned us to be disciples, not detectives. To be a student, not a spotter. To seek the healer, not the healing. To desire the Savior not the saving. The world undoubtedly calls us into the heavy tiresome work of a detective, while the light burden of Jesus calls us into the joy of discipleship. We often fall prey to satan's subtle, yet quite effective, tactic of finding-the-root instead of allowing our roots to reach far into His immeasurable life-giving water.

> *"Blessed are those who trust in the Lord and have made the Lord their hope and confidence. They are like trees planted along the riverbank, with roots that reach deep into the water. Such trees are not bothered by the heat or worried by long months of drought. Their leaves stay green, and they never stop producing fruit" (Jeremiah 17:7-8.)*

It's disciples who obtain a reverent heart and a satisfying internal rest; while detectives obtain a dangerous independent spirit and an exhausting internal burden. The detective spirit is doing the work of that which belongs solely to the Holy

Spirit, for He alone is the Perfect Detective who knows precisely which negative root must be located, eradicated and castrated at the very sound of His all-consuming, earth-shaking, intimately gentle voice. Daniel 2:47 describes my favorite title given of God: "The Revealer of Mysteries."

It's time we return the detective hat back to its Rightful Owner and believe every root driven far into His pure water, containing the complete and perfect remedy for each unwanted aliment, can be healed, will be restored, must be free. It's here where the "why's" behind our undesired behaviors, our negative thought patterns, our skewed belief systems, our relational failures; all become steps of falling north in our own personal sanctification journey with God, little by little. However, they are not the means of obtaining wholeness. Jesus is. Just Jesus-with or without the known cause of the root. The revealing of roots have never and will never bring intimacy with God. They're simply a byproduct of an already existing love walk with Him. We must first and foremost focus on the intimacy, obtained through the revolution of a reverent heart condition, rather than searching vigorously and exhaustedly for the negative/bad internal root. If there are bad roots, and there will be, trust that the all-sufficient, all-knowing, all-powerful, omnipresent, omniscient, omnipotent God can and will do that which we cannot.

Quite possibly we just need to get out of His way. And when we do, the most beautiful transaction in this particular step begins to emerge-the elimination, the evaporation, the eradication of *shame*. Shame is defined as, "A painful feeling of humiliation or distress caused by the conscious feeling of wrong or foolish behavior." We see in the book of Isaiah where he was brought before the holiness of God's throne, where he no doubt experienced the vast reverence and enormous awe-ness of His very presence. As a result, he naturally and unhesitatingly cried out, *"It's all over! I am doomed, for I am a sinful man. I have filthy lips, and I live among people with filthy lips. Yet I have seen the king, the Lord of Heaven's Armies"* (Isaiah 6:5.) God did something quite unexpected to Isaiah here. He sent an angel to touch his filthy lips with a coal potent enough to cleanse every residue of shame residing within his new reverent heart.

Because reverence kills shame.

Not only did God eradicate the former shame of Isaiah, He used the former shame of his mouth to become the very tool used to fulfill his purpose, his mission and his destination in his generation. Because, God often chooses to utilize our past mess as our current message. *"He touched my lips with it and said, "See this coal has touched your lips. Now your guilt is removed, and your sins are forgiven." Then I heard the Lord asking, "Whom should I send as a messenger to this people? Who will go for us? I said, "Here I am, send me."'* (Isaiah 6:7-8.)

However, satan, the accuser, desires nothing more than for us to not experience this life-giving, life-providing, life-altering, life-freeing reverence of Christ, simply because he has full knowledge that our internal life-zapping shame will undoubtedly melt in the glory of His presence. And that is why, dear friends, the greatest weapon in this very real spiritual battle is a daily practice of being in God's word and in His healing Light. It's here where we, day by day, offer to our generous, kind, forgiving, grace-filled, merciful, compassionate Father our mess-ups, our screw-ups and our cover-ups; all in order to beat satan to the punch. When we hide our sins, satan slithers right into the scene, implanting his shame filled messages deep into the walls of our soul.

"Then the angel showed me Jeshua, the high priest, standing before the angel of the Lord. The accuser, satan, was there at the angel's right hand making accusations against the priest. And the Lord said to satan, "I the Lord, reject your accusations, satan. Yes, the Lord, who has chosen Jerusalem, rebukes you. This man is like a burning stick that has been snatched from the fire." Jeshua's clothing was filthy as he stood there before the angel. So the angel said to the others standing there, "Take off his filthy clothes." And turning to Jeshua He said, "See, I have taken away your sins, and now I am giving you these fine new clothes"' (Zechariah 3:1-5.)

Jesus takes the clothing of our former filth, our former sin, our former shame and dresses us in dazzling, white, fine new clothing; presenting us before the watching world and in His sight as, "Holy and blameless as I stand before Him without a single fault" (Colossians 1:22.) It's not because we don't have faults; because if you're anything like me, they're too numerous to count. No friend, it's because in the Light of His presence, of His love, of His glory, of His kindness, of His blood, we are washed clean. Not based off of anything we have done or haven't done. Said or haven't said. Thought or haven't thought. Simply because of His undeserving, incomprehensible, unfathomable grace. Nothing more, nothing less.

Ironically, while writing this chapter, a sweet friend

texted me a verse which the Lord had given her on this particular morning. She felt she was to share it with me- and now, I'd like to share it with you:

*"But You, O Lord, are a shield around me; You are my glory, the **One who holds my head high**" (Psalm 3:3.)*

The weight of our former shame kept the position of our heavy heads facing low and south. Yet here, in the matchless beauty of Psalm 3:3, we're told it's only God who gently cups our face in the palms of His gentle hands while tilting the heart just slightly upward to gaze directly into His strong, potent, powerful, radiant, matchless and kind eyes. Eyes, without a word spoken, reveal His plan for our life is perfect. A plan revealing there is no ulterior route but to walk *through* the deep waters. *Through* the rivers of difficulty. *Through* the storms of oppression. *Through* the waves of doubt. Through. Yet, you dear friend, will not drown. You will not go under. You will not be engulfed in the waves—because God, who *is* enough, has parted the waters and is walking right along side you.

"But now, O Jacob, listen to the Lord who created you. O Israel, the One who formed you says, "Do not be afraid, for I have ransomed you. I have called you by name; you are mine. When you go through deep waters, I will be with you. When you go through rivers of difficulty, you will not drown. When you walk through the fire of oppression, you will not be burned up; the flames will not consume you. For I am the Lord, your God, the Holy One of Israel, Your Savior... Others were given in exchange for you. I traded their lives for yours because you are precious to me. You are honored, and

I love you. Do not be afraid, for I am with you. I will gather you and your children from east and west (Isaiah 43: 1-5.)

It's finally here, where our ears rest securely and safely on our Father's chest, actively listening for every faint whisper of His voice. A voice we know is not a voice of someone else who may have hurt, wounded, violated, rejected, betrayed or harmed our heart. No, this distinct voice comes from the lungs of the One who breathed new life into these former dry bones (Ezekiel 37: 4-5.) Reverent bones now dancing with vigorous joy and unashamed victory before the One who's very breath placed our hearts in a desirable reverent position of loving Him and others, "With all our heart, with all our soul, with all our strength, and with all our mind" (Luke 10:27.)

"But from everlasting to everlasting the Lord's Love is with those who fear Him, and His righteousness with their children's children."

Psalms 103:17

Questions to ponder with God

1. Is there a past memory/situation/event that might have tainted your ability to know and receive the love of God? If so, write it out and ask the Holy Spirit to reveal the lie you may have believed as your truth as a result of this relationship/event/trauma/etc.

2. Are you experiencing both the love of God and a deep reverence for Him? If so, what does this look like in your everyday life? If not, ask God to reveal what is holding you back from fully receiving and accepting this free-gift. Write out your thoughts below.

3. If you are struggling in this area, take some time to authentically write out a prayer asking God to enable you to be filled with the knowledge and experience of His transformational love, before moving on to the next chapter.

4. How is shame affecting your life today? Do you feel you've allowed God to eradicate its existence through the ingredient of a reverent heart towards Him? If not, what do you believe is preventing you from being free of it?

Scriptures

Exodus 4:31

Malachi 3:5-6

Psalm 103:11

2 Corinthians 7:1

Exodus 14:31

Psalm 119:116-120

1 Samuel 12:24

Micah 7: 15-18

Acts 9:31

Acts 10:35

Hebrews 12:28

What You're saying to me, God....

_____

_____

_____

_____

_____

_____

_____

_____

_____

_____

_____

_____

_____

_____

My prayer to You, Father....

_____

_____

_____

_____

_____

_____

_____

_____

_____

_____

_____

_____

_____

_____

_____

I can do All things through Christ

CHAPTER 4

REVERENCE = TRUST

"All who fear the Lord, trust the Lord!"
Psalm 115:11

It was the early spring of 2016. A spring season following that of a rough season, a persecution season, an in-just season, an unfair season, a hurtful season for my fifteen-year old first born girl. On this particular night, the lights were intensified, the cheering fans were chanting and the piercing sound of basketball shoes screeching the thickly glazed basketball court echoed off the high-school gymnasium walls and into the foundation of the bleachers where my husband and I sat watching the home basketball game. Yet, through the chattering and penetrating noise of the watching crowd, I noticed from the top row of our bleacher seat, *him* walk in.

Him, as in the boy who persecuted our daughter just months before through aggressive, purposeful, damaging and malicious words. He had a strong dis-like for a God he didn't know. A strong dis-like for those which followed Him. A strong dis-like for our girl he desired to date, yet couldn't due to her love for Jesus.

Yep, it was *him*.

Memories immediately flooding my thoughts to just months before, wrestling with how to seek justice for this young man's cruel words, hateful phone calls and daily verbal attacks towards our daughter. These days were filled with Jamie and I taking hands, pleading before the Lord to enable us to trust Him, hear Him, see Him above the noisy chatter of the many opinions of others as to what to do. Who to tell. How to protect. When to move.

Our baby girl being persecuted because of her faith in God was more than we could take most days, and my mama heart cried for justice. And yet, each time we brought our hurting spirit before the Lord, trusting Him for direction, we would collectively walk away with a confident-knowing He was unquestionably saying, "Be still."

And so, we did. We waited. We prayed. We cried; all the while being still in the deep, unshakeable trust that His love and protective instincts to care for our daughter superseded that of our own. However, this moment of watching the young man walk through the doors of the high school gymnasium ushered in the annoying reminder that justice had not yet been served, executed or completed to the level of justice my earthly flesh desired- and truthfully, desired from God. I felt the blood rush quickly into my face as I wavered between an internal battle of wanting to weep at the sight of this young man and yet longing to slug him one straight in the face. In an-effort to calm the intense emotions, I tried locking eyes with my husband, who was also on the top row of the gymnasium bleachers, but a few people down talking with a friend. As I sought Jamie's familiar eyes, I noticed he was no longer participating in his discussion. He, too, was now fixated on the sight of this young man standing down on the shiny gym floor.

That's when it happened.

Jamie slowly, yet intentionally stood up and began the long journey down the fifteen flights of bleachers, straight towards this young man near the entrance door. As much as I desired Jamie to take justice into his own hands, enable this young man to experience our pain, to know the level of hurt his words have caused, and to plead for our forgiveness, I knew any kind of scene would terribly embarrass our daughter and more importantly, would simply be an act of straight-up disobedience from what God asked us to do as we vowed and committed to trusting only in Him.

My heart rate increased with each increasing step Jamie made towards this boy. With one eye closed to pray and one eye open to witness that which was about to take place, I noticed something unpredictable, unnatural, something contrary to what I expected and ashamedly, desired. Jamie stood before this young man and with all intentionality, reached out his right arm and shook the boys hand, firmly yet respectfully. I noticed he shared a few brief words with the young man and deliberately walked straight back up to the top row of the bleachers.

As he approached the top row and proceeded to sit next to me, I looked over to him and inquired, "What was that?" He looked with puzzled eyes into mine and said, "I have no idea, Joy. I stood up to go down and tell that boy a few things, yet when I reached the second to last step I heard a **whisper** in my Spirit say, "Shake his hand and tell him something respectful." So, I did. I told him it was nice to see him and that my daughter has said nice things about him."

It's a quiet, small, tender whisper, isn't it? The trust whisper.

A whisper that's incongruent to a wandering thought, an unreliable feeling, a feeble desire and a clenched-gripped heart to seek justice for that which deserves punishment. This trust whisper, it opposes all reason, all rationale, all sensible and cognitive thinking. And yet, there it was. Undeniably camped out in the core of the heart, yet strangely quiet and persistently relentless.

A few days later as we were in the car together as a family, our daughter received a phone call from this young man. After answering, she began to repeat, "It's okay. I've already forgiven you, a long time ago. No, it's really okay. I promise. Of course, I forgive you." After hanging up she shared he was crying; broken over the fact he had hurt her with hateful words, wounded her with evil intentions and slandered her reputation due to her faith in God. The handshake he received the night at the basketball game gave him a glimpse and a taste of the make-no-sense kind of undeserved grace and kindness of Jesus. Where he deserved punishment, he was offered forgiveness. Where he deserved penalty, he was given freedom. Where he deserved justice, he was given grace. And as a result, it changed him, wrecked him forever.

As the preceding days, weeks, months went by, this young man began to inquire more about the God he witnessed in

Jamie's trust filled handshake. He began to have daily bible studies with our daughter, weekly youth group attendance at our local church and a new relationship with God in his every-day life. Which, in fact, all eventually led to his baptism last August in a lake behind my In-law's home. This young man, he's now a part of our extended family. One we love and care for a great deal. One we're honored to be witness to the restoration and redemption of a new life rooted in Christ. He now has a relationship with His True Father; a Father his orphan heart had longed and hungered for all along.

Had the gentle, unreasonable, make-no-sense kind of trust whisper been ignored on that Spring evening at the high school basketball game; hate and anger would of conquered. Yet, when obedience and a reverent heart desiring to fully embrace the very voice of a make-no-sense whisper to simply trust, grace and love prevailed. Hearts healed. Lives touched. Generations changed. Minds restored-all from the simplicity and the counter cultural obedience to a voice of an internal whisper. A whisper drenched of transforming power from the purest of lips whispering to simply trust Him.

But this trust thing, this internal whisper, this willful heart to respond to its absurd suggestion is *only* executed by the embedded, immovable, unshakeable secured knowing of Jesus' enough-ness. It's in this very knowing where our heart will begin to naturally metamorphosis itself into the beauty of an anchored trust, all while being in and under the Mighty hand of God.

"(V.6) Be humbled therefore under the mighty hand of God, so that He may exalt you in due

time,(ˇV.7) having cast all your anxiety on Him
(trusting Him,) because He cares for you."
1 Peter 5:6-7 BLB

Allow yourself to stay awhile in the center of this verse, while tuning the ears of the heart to pay close attention to the comma between verse 6 and 7. In some translations, this comma is often substituted by a period. However, the most accurate translation to its original Greek form in which Peter penned verses 6-7, the comma plays a key role in the distinction between a command and an outcome. A root and a fruit. A direction and a consequence. In other words, Peter is deliberately and passionately sharing with us that it's *impossible* to trust, to cast our anxiety on Him, unless we *first* humble ourselves under God's mighty hand. Do you see it? Do you recognize the significance of this small yet mighty passage? The command is *not* to trust. The command is *not* to cast our anxieties on Him. *The command is to humble ourselves under His mighty hand* (reverence) and then, and only then, can we cast our anxiety and trust Him.

Humbling ourselves under His mighty hand (reverence) is the root; casting anxiety (trust) is the fruit.

Humbling ourselves under His mighty hand is the command; casting anxiety is the outcome.

Humbling ourselves under His mighty hand is the direction; casting anxiety is the consequence.

Humbling ourselves under His mighty hand is the instruction; casting anxiety is the byproduct.

Reverence = Trust.

Can you picture Peter late one night, candle lit and pen in hand, sifting through imprinted memories of walking with Jesus, learning from Jesus, following Jesus, watching Jesus, listening to Jesus? He must of known the inmost details of Jesus' mighty hands. Every bump, bruise, vein, scar, color, texture. These same hands which reached out and pulled him from the raging sea beneath his feet. These same hands which gently placed a lifeless twelve-year old hand into His saying, "little one, get up!"

These same hands which passionately doodled in sand while angry stone-holders stared in confusion. These same hands which touched and healed the untouchable lesions of the leper. These same hands which brought life back to the dead bones of the paralyzed. These same hands used to gesture and emphasize His teaching of the parables with the masses. These same hands which touched the coffin of a widow's deceased son, supplying breath back into his lifeless lungs. These same hands which released demonic spirits, illnesses, diseases, and cured the blind (Luke 7:21.) These same hands which broke five loaves of bread and held up two fish to be multiplied by the power of God. These same hands which embraced tender little children climbing up onto His lap. These same hands which took bread and gave thanks to God saying, "This is my body, which is given for you. Do this in remembrance of me." These same hands used to wash and dry off the feet of His disciples. These same hands used to wipe away drops off blood dripping from His sweat glands moments before His arrest. These same hands which were nailed, beaten and whipped so that we could be whole and healed (Isaiah 53:5.)

Peter knew His hands, therefore he knew something that we may not know-- in order for us to cast our anxieties, to release our worries, to relinquish our fears, to surrender our lives, to *trust* God, we must *first* know the *mighty-ness* of <u>His hand</u> in which He is holding us securely in. Ironically, this same description of Gods mighty hand is intimately sewn, deliberately intertwined and passionately interwoven throughout all sixty-six books of His Word. A small sampling of this includes:

His protection: "He has hidden me in the shadow of <u>His hand.</u>" Isaiah 49:2.

His parental love: "I have written your name on the palms of <u>My hands.</u>" Isaiah 49:16.

His generosity: "The <u>gracious hand</u> of the Lord God is on me." Ezra 7:28.

His mercy: "All day long I have held out <u>My hands</u> to an obstinate people, who walk in ways not good, pursuing their own imagination." Isaiah 65:2.

His security: "And I have put My words in your mouth and hidden you safely in <u>My hand.</u>" Isaiah 51:16.

His authorship: "Didn't <u>My hands</u> make both heaven and earth?" Acts 7:50.

His strength: "Strong is Your arm! Strong is <u>Your hand</u>! Your <u>right hand</u> is lifted high in glorious strength." Psalm 89:13.

His leadership: "My future is in <u>Your hands</u>." Psalm 31:15.

His position: "You are our Father. We are the clay, and you are the potter. We all are formed by <u>Your hand.</u>" Isaiah 64:8.

His creatorship: "Who else has held the oceans in <u>His hand</u>? Who has measured off the heavens with His fingers?" Isaiah 40:12.

His sufficiency: "When You open <u>Your hand</u>, You satisfy the hunger and thirst of every living thing." Psalm 145:16.

His pride: "The Lord will hold you in <u>His hand</u> for all to see. A splendid crown <u>in the hand of God.</u>" Isaiah 62:3.

His light: "His coming is as brilliant as the sunrise. Rays of light flash from <u>His hands</u> where his awesome power is hidden." Habakkuk 3:4.

His justice: "Though I walk in the midst of trouble, You will revive me; You will stretch forth <u>Your hand</u> against the wrath of my enemies, and Your <u>right hand</u> will save me." Psalm 138:7.

His discipline: "For your arrows have sunk deep into me. And <u>Your hand</u> has pressed down on me." Psalm 38:2.

His victory: "Sing a new song to the Lord, for He has done wonderful deeds. His <u>right hand</u> has won a mighty victory; His holy arm has shown His saving power." Psalm 98:1.

His redemption: "You redeemed by Your great power and by Your <u>strong hand.</u>" Nehemiah 1:10.

His help: "Do not be afraid, for I am with you. Don't be discouraged for I am your God. I will strengthen and help you. I will hold you up with my victorious <u>right hand.</u>" Isaiah 41:10.

His provision: "My Father has given them to me, and He is more powerful than anyone else. No one can snatch them from the <u>Father's hand</u>." John 10:29.

His grace: "Who then will condemn us? No one- for Christ Jesus died for us, and He is sitting in the place of honor at God's <u>right hand</u>, pleading for us." Romans 8:34.

This tender, yet mighty hand is no small matter. His fastened hand is what reaches *through* the web of our chaos, *through* the quick sand of our impending trial, *through* the iron wall of our painful past, *through* the drowning water of our current circumstance, *through* the entangled mess of our relationships and *through* the prison bars of our heightened emotions. His powerful right arm reaches through; not above, or below, or around, but *through,* in order for us to get-to. Positioning our weary souls to be tightly held and tenderly carried (Isaiah 63:9) by the Mighty-Hand of our Papa while experiencing the rushing waves of His life-altering security and a steady river of His peace (Isaiah 66:12.)

Yet, Isaiah 51:5 tells us, "...*All distant lands will look to me and <u>wait in hope</u> for my powerful arm.*" Because, there's some waiting in the trust, isn't there? Maybe that's why we're forewarned repetitively in Apostle Paul's letters to pray for patient-endurance. Admittedly, both these words make me uncomfortable. And yet, Paul, in all His Godly wisdom knew in advance that in-order for us to trust, while waiting in hope, we'd have to armor ourselves with the necessary ingredient of patient endurance.

Because: trust=waiting in hope.

Here's just a small sampling of God's word confirming and reminding and equipping and preparing our weary hearts to wait-in-hope while in this love walk of trust with our Good Father:

Isaiah 51:5: "My mercy and justice are coming soon. My salvation is on the way. My strong arm will bring justice to the nations. All distant lands will look for me and <u>wait-in-hope</u> for my powerful arm."

Psalm 40:1: "I <u>waited patiently</u> for the Lord to help me and He turned to me and heard my cry."

Psalm 37:7: "Be still in the presence of the Lord, and <u>wait patiently</u> for Him to act."

Isaiah 30:18: "So the Lord must wait for you to come to Him so He can show you His love and compassion. For the Lord is a faithful God. Blessed are those who <u>wait for His help</u>."

Jeremiah 14:22: "Can any of the worthless foreign gods send us rain? Does it fall from the sky by itself? No, You are the One, O Lord our God! Only You can do such things. So we will <u>wait for You</u> to help us."

Psalm 25:5: (NIV) "Lead me in Your truth and teach me, for You are the God of my salvation; For You <u>I wait all the day.</u>"

Psalm 33:20: (NIV) "Our soul <u>waits for the Lord</u>; He is our help and our shield."

Psalm 130:5: (NIV) "I <u>wait for the Lord</u>, my soul does <u>wait.</u> And in His Word do I hope."

Micah 7:7: "As for me, I look to the Lord for help. <u>I wait confidently</u> for God to save me, and my God will certainly hear me."

Isaiah 8:17: "I will <u>wait for the Lord</u> who has turned away from the descendants of Jacob. I will put my hope in Him."

Psalm 39:7: (NIV) "And now, Lord, for what do <u>I wait?</u> My hope is in You."

Luke 12:37: "The servants who are ready and <u>waiting</u> for His return will be rewarded."

Romans 8:23: "And we believers also groan even though we have the Holy Spirit within us as a foretaste of future glory, for we long for our bodies to be released from sin and suffering. We <u>wait with eager hope</u> for the day when God will give us our full rights as His adopted children, including the new bodies He has promised us."

Hebrews 9:28: "So also Christ offered once for all time as a sacrifice to take away the sins of many people. He will come again, not to deal with our sins, but to bring salvation to all who are eagerly <u>waiting for Him</u>."

Psalm 62:5: "Let all that I am <u>wait quietly </u>before God, for my hope is in Him."

It's in this waiting, in this gap, where what we've left behind and what's to come has yet to take fruition. And yet, because doubt and despair and hopelessness and fear often become our greatest temptations during these seasons of wait, God has hand planted specific truths in His word to encourage and strengthen our fearful souls. One of these truths, which I've often parked my own heart at during seasons of being in the middle, is Isaiah 49:15:

> *"Never! Can a mother forget her nursing child? Can she feel no love for the child she has borne? But even if that were possible, I would not forget about you! See, I have written your name on the palms of my hands…"*

Recognize here in this Isaiah verse, God doesn't only say, "A mother," but a, "Nursing mother." Why? Because even if a mother could forget her child emotionally, mentally, spiritually- for a nursing mother, physically, it is near impossible. Her body will involuntarily begin to develop and expel milk at the sound of a newborns cry and at repetitive time periods through-out the day. Physiologically, it is *impossible* for God to forget you. To not love you.

Impossible.

And because of this impossibility, based off of nothing you have done or have not done to deserve or not deserve His love, a resolved reverent heart begins to emerge, enabling our spirit to *naturally trust*. A trust where we know the One to whom is holding our life, binding our life and protecting our life. The One to whom we know has no lacks, has no wants, has no gaps, has no cracks, has no holes. The One who is the Beginning and the End. The First and the Last. The Alpha and the Omega. The Keeper and the Creator. The Author and the Architect. The Counselor and the Physician. The Father and the Friend. The Anchor and the Hope. The Comforter and the Healer. The One who Is and who Was and who Is to come. The One who, "When the Israelites *saw* the mighty hand of the Lord displayed against the Egyptians, feared the Lord, and *as a result*, placed their trust in Him" (Exodus 14:31 NIV.)

God's life-giving, shame-eradicating, freedom-supplying Light (Luke 11:35) enables all to be exposed, all to be revealed, all to be known, all to be felt-so that we can deliberately transfer each of the heavy morsels of our soul, with our limited shaking palms, into His mighty, sufficient, stable, peace-supplying, joy-in-abundance hand. A hand which is now firmly trusted deep in our belief system as the Rock, the Shelter, the Safe Haven, the Security; the *only* Mighty hand equipped and able to do that which appears impossible, from a God who is and does the impossible (Luke 1:37.)

"God's hand never slips. He never makes a mistake. His every move is for our own good and for our ultimate good."
-Billy Graham

Questions to ponder with God

1. Read Mark 4:39-41. Why did the disciples have little trust and faith in Jesus' ability to stop the storm? (answer in verse 41.)

2. Have you ever been told to simply trust God more, and yet unable to do so? Write down your experience.

3. How do you feel knowing that trusting Jesus is a natural by-product of a reverent heart towards Him? How will/could this potentially change your relationship with Him?

4. Do you recognize the Mighty Hand of God operating in your own life? If so, how?

Scriptures

Psalm 115:11

Isaiah 33:17

Jeremiah 17:7-8

Psalm 9:10

Romans 15:13

Isaiah 33:6

Galatians 3:6-9

Proverbs 19:23

Isaiah 30:20-23

Isaiah 35:4

Psalm 119:38

What You're saying to me, God....

_____

_____

_____

_____

_____

_____

_____

_____

_____

_____

_____

_____

_____

_____

My prayer to You, Father....

_____

_____

_____

_____

_____

_____

_____

_____

_____

_____

_____

_____

_____

_____

I will walk by faith

CHAPTER 5

TRUST = JOY

*"My heart is confident in you, O God; no wonder
I can sing your praises with all my heart!*
Psalm 108:1

Fighting the fierce fight of a rare blood cancer, my mom gently led my hand into hers. With tear-filled eyes locking a strong gaze with the eyes of my heart, she spoke ten words which punctured through this very moment in time we were sharing on her sunroom couch.

"Just because I'm crying, doesn't mean I don't have joy."

Yes, sweet Mama, "You're most definitely right," I whispered to myself.

A heart overflowing with painful grief,
can still be a heart overflowing with anchored faith.

A heart consumed with tragic loss,

can still be a heart consumed with incomprehensible hope.

A heart flooded with threatening fear,
can still be a heart flooded with unfathomable trust.

A heart absorbed with deep implanted sadness,
can still be a heart absorbed with boundless joy.

It's here, while in the unwanted valley of life, she's developing a new normal. An internal Godly security drawing the truth of Habakkuk 3:17-19 to be a steadfast reality in the deepest reservoir of the heart within.

> *"<u>Even-though</u> the fig trees have no blossoms and there are no grapes on the vines; <u>even-though</u> the olive crops fail and the fields lie empty and barren; <u>even-though</u> the flocks die in the fields, and the cattle barns are empty, I will rejoice in the Lord! I will be joyful in the God of my salvation! The sovereign Lord is my strength! He makes me as surefooted as a deer, able to tread upon the heights."*

Even though.

As I peal back the former pages of my own life containing doses of pain, seasons of suffering, moments of wounding, pangs of hurt, times of loss and chapters of grief, I recognize, ashamedly, a dangerous pattern of thinking. A type of thinking in which the enemy polluted and trespassed on the grounds of my thoughts while carelessly tossing rotting garbage bags of hopelessness and despair in every available corner of the mind. Resulting in:

My lips speaking, "God, you're my refuge."
My thoughts whispering, "God, where are you?"

My lips speaking, "God, You're all powerful."
My thoughts whispering, "God, You've forgotten about me."

My lips speaking, "God, Your love is enough."
My thoughts whispering, "God, I need something more."

My lips speaking, "God, Your plan is perfect."
My thoughts whispering, "God, You need my help."

Until, that is, the band aid of my imitation, life-less, joy-depleted faith slipped off the open sores of the heart, revealing battle wounds of former loss, past grief, stuffed pain and repressed hurt. All, still in their original form, yet now toxic, infected and *smothered* in shame. But here's the thing, we have an enemy who strategically deceives and craftily convinces the mind that these raw God-given emotions simply are incongruent to that of a follower of Jesus. When in fact, God systematically chooses to use these very real ingredients of suffering to draw the damaged and trust-lacking heart straight to the One and Only Healer-the Physician who specializes in turning former mourning into unspeakable joy, saying;

"Their life will be like a watered garden, and all their
sorrows will be gone. The young women will dance
for joy, and the men- old and young- will join in the
celebration. I will turn their mourning into joy. I will
comfort them and exchange their sorrow for rejoicing."

(Jeremiah 31:12-13.)

And, "To all who mourn, He will give a crown of beauty for ashes, a **joyous** blessing instead of mourning, a festive praise instead of despair. In their righteousness, they will be like a great oak tree that the Lord has planted for His own glory. Instead of shame and dishonor, you will enjoy a double share of honor. You will possess a double portion of prosperity, and everlasting **joy** will be yours." (Isaiah 61:3,7.)

But, maybe, just possibly this one trouble, the big-one in our life is being used to make us, not break us. To refine us, not define us. Could it be this very trouble is the sole ingredient God is using to position the heart to be catapulted into receiving our purpose, our calling, our joy?

Because when our faith is tested, only through a trial such as this, endurance has an opportunity to grow. And when endurance is fully developed, God says we are, "Perfect and complete, lacking nothing" (James 1.4.) Yet, we cannot obtain completeness and lacking-nothing-ness, unless we first have a trouble, a temptation, a heartache, a tribulation, a trust-tester. Come to find out, what the enemy intended to destroy us, to harm us, to scare us, to deplete us of joy, of peace, of hope, and of trust, is the very thing God uses to complete us. To fill us. To make us. To beautify us.

I've found I'm often searching for comfort while God is instilling character. Often searching for wavering happiness while God is infusing stable joy. Often searching for placidity while God is establishing purpose. Yet it's here, in such a time as this, knee high in grief, in confusion, in fear, in doubt, in pain-where the Creator, the Maker, the Perfect One pours His love into the reservoir of our trust tank, filling, overflowing, ushering in, "Perfection and completeness and the lack of nothing" (James 1:4.)

As I continually witness Christ supernaturally pour both His strength and joy into my mom, I'm forced to examine the intricate details of the xray of my own joy tank. What if I chose to not cover up my perceived weakness so that Gods power, Gods strength, God's *joy* can be perfected in me? In all its beauty, all its power, for all to see; so that *when,* not if, He heals, comforts, supplies, strengthens-the evidence of a confident hope and a steadfast joy can only be recognized as *His* magnificent work and not my own (Judges 7:2.) For my inadequacies, my flaws, my weaknesses are too significant for such a strength, for such a transformation, for such an ecstatic abundance of joy blanketing that of my former gloom.

Even knowing this, it's a daily discipline to allow God the access within to fight against the temptation of living an illusion, a mirage, a false-reality, a fake-joy for the convincing of both myself and others. God simply desires honesty, often times messy, yet honest. The messy portion is God's favorite, wouldn't you agree? It's His open gateway into our fragile lives, shining His perfection into our messiness while supplying breaths of refreshment into that which is parched for life-giving, purified, transforming, radiating, genuine, exceeding joy.

Messy honesty no longer needs to be bound in secret, avoided and silenced; yet embraced, shared, released into the mighty hands of the One who kindly smiles confidently in the face of our internal ugly. Knowing it's in this messy honesty where we satisfactorily taste His never-be-the-same kind of transformational joy. It's where our inadequacies are celebrated, His strength is activated and new victorious joy is experienced. Trust is the key which unlocks this delightful doorway of joy. A joy, carefully administered by the Holy Spirit (Galatians 5:22,) yet easily suffocated by the persistent worries, the relentless concerns and the heavy burdens of everyday life. Joy follows trust simply because the mighty hand of God, discussed in the previous chapter, raises the unbearable weight, lifts the relentless worry, and eradicates the persistent anxiety. His refreshing hope has been restored and the immovable anchor has been deeply implanted; all for the move-that-bus moment of our former withered soul to reveal its God given gift of *inexpressible joy*.

I have an esteemed love and deep appreciation for those who refurbish, restore and refinish seasoned furniture. Stripping the deformities, sanding the grain, applying the stain, administering the sealer-all one patient layer at a time. It's a detailed process involving commitment, sacrifice and dedication to remove the multiple decades of weathered tear in-order for watching eyes to see that which had been seen all along by its restorer-the radiating and originally designed beauty underneath. Our lives are often like these delicately constructed antique pieces of furniture. Once illuminating with beauty and purpose, yet now coated in multiple layers of worry, anxiety, fear. All of which were causing the joy of His Spirit to be dulled and blanketed by the multiple layered burdens of this world.

And yet His truth tells me He hears and rescues when I call to Him for help (Psalm 34:17.) He is close to the broken-hearted and rescues those whose spirits are crushed (Psalm 34:18.) He does not ignore the cries of those who suffer (Psalm 9:12.) He is a shelter for those who are weighed down with burden, pain, hurts, wounding, grief and loss (Psalm 91:2.) He is a refuge in times of trouble (psalm 9:9.) He restores, supports, strengthens and places our weary feet on a firm foundation. (1Peter 5:10.) He is our strength and shield; enabling the heart to trust Him fully and to be filled with *joy* (Psalm 28:7.)

There is no greater a privilege than to be witness to that of a brave and courageous soul who purposefully, willfully, deliberately and obediently chooses God as the One and Only method of comfort, *while in-the-pain*. The rough stripping, the deep refining, the continual sanding of one's life back to its original and former beauty is not for the faint of heart. To boldly swim against the fierce rugged tides of the worlds system, all while being persistently tempted, aggressively lured and craftily deceived by the enemy that there's an easier route, a quicker fix, a better way *around-the-pain* instead of *remaining-in-the-pain* with Jesus, takes a courage beyond that of our limited humanness. Yet, joy, in its rarest and purest form is found when the faulty and easily deceived fragile heart is given divine access to receive the boundless, the unequaled, the matchless, the enormous privilege of being under the provision and protection of God's mighty hand, all while enduring the fiercest of storms.

It's in-the-pain where we can tenderly and intimately feast on the raw, undiluted joy of God's unequivocal presence (Psalm 16:11) and *mighty hand*. A hand which lifts the inmost mourning and transfers it into outmost dancing. A hand which releases consistent despair and replaces it with imbedded hope. A hand which loosens delicate weakness and redeems it into unbreakable strength. A hand which unbinds oppressive pain and restores it into cheerful joy. It's here, under the safety, provision and love of God's Presence where joy unspeakable restores the sparkle of the eye (Psalm 13:3.)

In the book of Ezra, the Israelites were given permission to return to their home land and rebuild their former beloved and cherished temple. This Holy temple was devastatingly destroyed just 60 short years prior and was originally designed by the wisest, richest, most powerful man of all time, King Solomon. It lacked absolutely nothing. The finite details, the overlaid gold walls, the precisely placed jewels, the hand-crafted carvings-- the intricacy of every corner was stunningly, radiantly and breathtakingly magnificent. It surpassed anything of its kind in all the world.

However, this holy temple of the Israelites was completely destroyed by an enemy. Torn down, knocked down, belittled, betrayed, rejected and desecrated beyond repair. Can you relate? Is that which God built in your life, with His own hands, gone? Taken? Could this temple represent what was once beautiful, sacred, significant, precious in your life? Possibly a marriage, a childhood, a family, a career, a ministry, a person, a relationship, a dream. Did an enemy unwelcomingly bolt in without an inkling of permission and violate, trash, disregard this holy and sacred place of your heart, eventually tearing it down to the original dirt lying just underneath its former foundation?

You're not alone. The Israelites, too, experienced this level of sorrow, of heartache, of loss, of pain, of grief, of devastation. And yet, God, in all His goodness, did what He does best: **resurrect.** Eventually, stirring the hearts of those He chose to rebuild what was formerly abolished, (Ezra 1:5) He began to resurrect their new temple--a new marriage, a new dream, a new childhood, a new relationship, a new normal. *"All the people gave a great shout, praising the Lord because the new foundation of the Lord's temple had been laid. But many of the older priests, Levites, and other leaders who had seen the first temple wept aloud when they saw the new Temple's foundation. The others, however, were shouting for joy. <u>The joyful shouting and weeping mingled together</u> in a loud noise that could be heard far in the distance"* (Ezra 3:11-13.)

As we begin to witness God re-construct, resurrect, and redeem a new foundation in our lives, our hearts naturally remember the old. We weep in sorrow for that which was lost, yet shout for joy for that which is re-built. A new temple. A new relationship. A new career. A new hope. A new dream. A new chapter. A new season. It's where our joy and our weeping are "mingled together" in a loud noise which can be heard far in the distance of the heart.

Our very being is purposefully, intricately and delicately designed to experience the *opposites* of both pain and Joy. It's here in the middle of these two opposing emotions where Jesus crawls into our chaos and unravels the mess. Organizes the confusion. Irons out the heartache. Administers His comfort. Resurrects the new.

It's in this position where we allow the Master Architect, the Qualified Builder of our hearts access into the internal mess. With His unaltered blue print, His unvarying plumb line and His unfailing design, He enables the heart to embrace the steadfastness of His encompassing love while cleaving to the hope of the new temple within. It's in the pain, in the suffering, in the heartache where the joy is found by our Matchless Maker, our Faultless Father and our Compassionate Compass who has a plan which will not be thwarted, prevented or obstructed (Job 42:2.) Because it's in the heartache, we find the joy (2 Corinthians 6:10.)

"Joy is not necessarily the absence of suffering, it's the presence of God."
-Sam Storms

Questions to Ponder with God

1. Have you experienced a season of both joy and pain? If so, write about this time in your life.

2. Have you found it easier to stuff your pain and to fake joy?

3. Are you willing to walk-through-the pain with Christ, instead of around-the-pain, in-order to experience His joy?

4. Write out a prayer inviting the Holy Spirit into your pain, while releasing your fears, your shame, your hurt into His mighty hands with an expectant heart to receive His joy.

Scriptures

<u>1 Peter 1:8-9</u>

<u>Nehemiah 8:10</u>

<u>Psalm 30:11</u>

<u>Psalm 126:6</u>

<u>Psalm 30:5</u>

Isaiah 35:10

Isaiah 61:7

John 16:24

Romans 5:1-5

John 16:22

Psalm 94:19

What You're saying to me, God....

_____

_____

_____

_____

_____

_____

_____

_____

_____

_____

_____

_____

_____

_____

_____

My prayer to You, Father....

_____

_____

_____

_____

_____

_____

_____

_____

_____

_____

_____

_____

_____

_____

_____

He will

restore

my soul

CHAPTER 6

JOY = SURRENDER

Trust in the Lord with all your heart, do not depend on your own understanding. Seek His will in all you do and He will show you which path to take."
Proverbs 3:5

Almost immediately I came to the stark realization there's no such thing as cruise control in marriage.

It poured on our wedding day. Buckets of hail. Torrential rain. Un-drivable flooding. Bolts of lightning. Earth-shaking thunder. We lost electricity during the ceremony more times than I can count, greeted with strikes of piercing lightning radiating the dark sanctuary with sharp and sudden flashes of light in between the vows and ring exchange. The Redford Observer's next morning cover story stated that June 12, 1999 was the largest storm in over twenty years.

Quite possibly, this was an indicator and/or a direct reflection of the storms which were to lie ahead. And it was apparent, almost instantaneously, the enemy was after our marriage the exact moment we said our I-do's. He was going to stop at nothing to tear apart that which God had placed together. He recognized, much more than Jamie and I had fully comprehended at the time, the power, the force, the severe impact we, as a married union, could have for a hundred generations.

Had I known what I humbly comprehend now, I would of seen the reality behind God's original blue print when He ordained, designed and implemented marriage. I recognize marriage was originated so that we could be an accurate representation of His security, His devotion, His faithfulness, His protection, His character, His power, His kindness and His unconditional love to one another.

And yet, the enemy, who desires nothing more than to destroy marriages, has full insight to the generational impact and effectiveness of a married couple. He relentlessly and tirelessly pursued our marriage, stopping at nothing until he caused enough strife, hostility, dissension, division, anger, bitterness, un-forgiveness, rejection, wounding, deceit and betrayal for us to fling our hands in the air and say his three favorite words which bring twisted music to his dark and wicked ears; **"I give up."** It was then, in this moment, he smiled his repulsive grin and slithered away fully satisfied, for his only objective was to kill, steal and destroy (John 10:10.)

From day one of our marriage, he caused quarreling, he planted discord, he encouraged disagreements, he generated disputes, he induced strife, he introduced chaos and produced confusion. It soon became a repetitive and habitual response to our everyday living. The core foundation of the marriage cracked just slightly open with each repetitive argument--flooding in buckets of mistrust, judgements, assumptions, jealousy, control, manipulation, fear and insecurity, to name a few.

Little did we know how viciously and maliciously we were being hunted-down. **Instead of recognizing the true-enemy, we looked and saw only each other as the villain.** Satan took pure delight in watching the debris and the aftermath remnants of our parental arguments being poured over, fallen onto and seeped into the tender hearts of our children. He purposefully strived to cause debilitating instability, crippling fear, constant confusion, on-going mistrust and deep-seeded-wounding into their sweet little identities.

Nothing brought him greater twisted joy than to watch Jamie and I argue over words, stature, control, ownership, authority, rights and wounded emotions. Pride fueled the arguing and selfishness drove it straight into a brick wall, every time. As if it were yesterday, I turned the corner, after a grueling argument of selfish motives, hurtful words and hateful gestures, to see my five-year old daughter clinging to the stairwell post with tears streaming down her rosy button cheeks. As I wiped away the blonde strands of her long thick hair sticking to her tear drenched neck, she looked at me with her perfectly round, blue, innocent eyes and whispered, "It scares me when you fight with daddy. I'm scared Mommy." It was in that moment I came to a life-altering recognition that nothing has more of an effectual power to shake the very foundation of a child's security than that of quarreling parents.

I recognize now it was a heart condition which hadn't fully known or trusted God when I chose to argue rather than bring it to Him-- my True Counselor (Isaiah 9:6) my

Great Physician (Mark 2:17) my Guardian of my soul (1 Peter 2:25.) I simply and naively didn't believe in His authority to eradicate darkness, to provide healing, to remove brokenness, to eliminate pride, to destroy selfishness, to snap chains, to massage a hardened heart, to fill in the cracks, to comfort the pain. And, as a result, I'd step in and play His divine role to change my spouse-- when in reality, it was I who needed a heart transformation.

The changing of my husband's heart never went as I desired it to go, simply because it was never my burden to bear, or repair. Even with my well-thought-out ideas and well-put-together plans and well-structured-boundaries, it failed to succeed. Every time. Day after day, week after week, month after month and year after year, this exhausting cycle continued. God loved me too much to allow my own deceitful heart to be masked by the deception of denial and control. I found it considerably easier to point a finger outward than to allow His Light to reveal and expose that which was broken within me, ultimately leading the heart to *surrender.*

I wanted to be heard. To be understood. To be empathized. To be consoled. To be whatever the need of my heart may have been in the moment. And when it wasn't provided, whether deserved or not, I was willing to fight for it regardless of the damage it was causing the little ears listening. We were both participating in adult temper tantrums resulting in generational harm to not only our own lives, but to every person in our sphere who loved us, depended on us, looked to us, relied on us; especially the little-one's who'd been entrusted into our care.

I finally held up a white flag and *surrendered* myself before the Only One who was capable of performing heart surgery-*Jesus*. After too many attempts to even admit, I finally grasped, through utter exhaustion, that I was significantly under qualified to change another's heart, including my own. This wasn't an overnight process. In fact, it was day by day by day by day....

With each new morning, I'd crawl my weary body, broken heart and shattered spirit into His all-consuming, peace-filled, love-oozing presence, where He'd *never* fail to nurture my breached soul, feed my confused mind and console my burdened heart. It was here, in the simplicity, in the humility and in the calmness of intimacy with Christ, in which my heart was immersed in His life-supplying joy. My Spirit was refreshed. My mind was reprogrammed. My heart was restored. My soul was surrendered.

It's here in this particular phase of Joy=Surrender, where forgiveness is naturally poured out to those we once found impossible to forgive. When our tired, yet dancing-with-joy feet enter this transformational doorway of surrender, we walk in with the deep abiding knowing we have been fully, completely, radically and undeservingly forgiven by the One who sent His son to die for that which deserved punishment. Yet, instead, we were given love. Given grace. Given mercy. Given forgiveness. Given life. It's simply due to experiencing and being filled in abundance with this undeserved forgiveness of God, which now enables us to fully and supernaturally forgive those who we've been asked and encouraged to forgive. This simple, yet mighty act is done from a genuine motive, a sincere heart, an internal pull resulting from receiving that which had been given freely and undeservingly to us, "In full, pressed down, shaken together to make room for more, running over, and poured into our lap" (luke 6:38.)

It's right here, right now, in this place, where we *surrender* three key areas of our lives into the hands of our Mighty God:

1. Our Minds.
2. Our Body.
3. Our Will.

Our mind:

Since what is repeated is reinforced, our minds are often both programmed and polluted with lies through past violations, wounds, unmet needs, betrayals and/or rejections-all of which stitch thick cords of unworthiness and invaluableness in and through the core of our belief system. Romans 12:2 tell us, *"Do not conform to the pattern of this world, but be transformed by the renewing of your mind. Then you will be able to test and approve what God's will is—His good, pleasing and perfect will."*

In other words, it's impossible to know our distinct purpose, to receive our fulfilling destination, to acknowledge our perfect will while still operating in a faulty belief system of the mind. God desires not to simply change *what* we think, but *how* we think. *How* we think of Him. *How* we think of ourselves. *How* we think of our worth, our value, our calling, our purpose. It's in the *How*, where we'll find our freedom. Philippians 4:6 says, *"Don't worry about anything. Instead, pray about everything. Tell God what you need, and thank Him for all He has done. Then you will experience God's peace, which exceeds anything we can understand. His peace will guard your hearts and* **minds** *as you live in Christ Jesus."*

Surrendering both our hearts and minds to Him through prayer, moment by moment, enables the beauty of His intimacy (into-me-see) to heal the damaged and poisonous faulty thinking. When we begin to take on the mind of Christ (Philippians 2:5,) we begin to recognize the damaging lies for what they are-an erroneous deception straight from the pit of hell. Little by little, Jesus begins to eradicate these dysfunctional, inaccurate and paralyzing beliefs, while simultaneously replacing them with His truths and naturally ushering in purpose, provision and protection to our very souls.

Our body:

I remember distinctly hearing the voice of God just days leading up to my spinal surgery, penetratingly whispering deep in the heart of my spirit. This voice assured me that the entire purpose of this surgery was to glorify Him. Bottom line. No exceptions. It was not about the outcome. It was not about the surgeon. It was not about my own fears and/ or hopes. It was simply about Him getting glory through it all. And because of this knowing, as I slipped my handwritten letters under each pillow of my sleeping babies that early march morning hour of my surgery, I remember fully, completely and resolvedly surrendering my body to God. If this surgery meant losing my life, I repeated, "I am willing."

Because it was in that moment where six words remained fresh on my surrendered heart- "This surgery is to glorify Him." And If glorifying God, which I believed was the entire purpose of my existence, meant the absence of this human tent from this fallen world of that which I have known—then I was willing.

"I plead with you to give your bodies to God because of all He has done for you. Let them be a living and holy sacrifice- the kind He will find acceptable. This is truly the way to worship Him"
(Romans 12:1.)

"Don't you realize that your body is the temple of the Holy Spirit, who lives in you and was given to you by God? You do not belong to yourself, for God bought you with a high price. So you must honor God with your body"
(1 Corinthians 3:16-17.)

"For whoever wants to save his life will lose it, but whoever loses his life for me will save it. What good is it for a man to gain the whole world, and yet lose or forfeit his very soul?"
(Luke 9:24-25.)

"Take up your cross (be willing to surrender our life) and follow me"
(Matthew 16:24.)

Offering our bodies to God each day, knowing we are His and He is ours- both enables and encourages us to use our bodies as living and power-infused vessels, vehicles and instruments of His unfathomable glory. As we crawl up into His secure and strong and compassionate and merciful presence each morning, we are undoubtedly reminded of the inherent worth and value and treasure He sees when His eyes lock gaze with ours. In this, we are displaying the ultimate act of surrender and sacrifice, both holy and pleasing to God— "Our true and proper worship" (Romans 12:1 NIV.)

Our will:

When our daughter was in the 5th grade, we had a pool party for her 10th birthday. Unbeknownst to us, one of the young girls attending the party did not know how to swim, nor did she desire to share this vital information with myself or any of the other children at the party. In the hidden thoughts of her mind, she decided she was safe hanging-out in the shallow end. This way, nobody had to know her secret. Unfortunately, however, our pool was a sports pool, which simply meant the shallow end was minimal and short, while the deep end took up the majority of the pool. As you can suspect, one step too far and she was drowning. As much as this sweet girl wanted her life to be saved in this moment, it was out of her control to save herself. She required a buoy. A life-guard. A savior. Something and/or someone outside herself who could rescue her from the flooding waters dragging her down deep below the pool's surface. Immediately, my oldest son took action and yelled loudly for her to grab hold of the blue pool noodle held tightly and firmly in the grip of his right hand. She was willing, as she reached her arm out from the heavy waters consuming her body and took hold while being pulled down towards the shallow end where safety and security and life were waiting for her.

Often, Jesus, just moments before He rescued, healed and/or saved one of His precious children, He'd ask, "Are you willing?" Jesus fully knew they were drowning in the flood waters of life and were unable to save themselves; and yet He still asked, "Are you willing?" And, truthfully, He's actively asking the same of you and me today, *"Are we willing?"* Are we willing to let Him walk with us during the pain of suffering? Are we willing to let go of our counterfeit peanut butters? Are we willing to receive His immovable love? Are we willing to revere Him in all His unfathomable glory? Are we willing to trust in His strangely quiet relentless whisper? Are we willing to receive His unspeakable joy? Are we willing to surrender our mind, body and will?

Are you willing?

If so, His only requirement is for us to lift-up our arm through the heavy drowning waters of our circumstances and grab hold of His life-giving hand.

A hand which will enable us to:
Let go of past pain
Let go of haunting fear
Let go of un-forgiveness
Let go of toxic bitterness
Let go of counterfeit comforts
Let go of festering shame
Let go of deep rooted lies
Let go of inner vows

Let go of lies
Let go of control
Let go of negative thinking
Let go of idolatry
Let go of codependency
Let go of hate
Let go of assumptions
Let go of addictions
Let go of insecurity
Let go of false guilt
Let go of perfectionism
Let go of anger
Let go of judgement
Let go of manipulation
Let go of selfishness
Let go of legalism
Let go of envy
Let go of pride.

Do you feel it? The yoke is being lifted. His love rushing over you, cleansing you, purifying you, cleaning you, redeeming you from the inside out. Infusing you with the cure. Administering you with the antidote. Supplying you with the remedy. Permeating you with the answer. Implanting you with the key to life (Revelation 1:8.) From this knowledge, this understanding, this assurance, letting go/surrendering becomes a natural, joyful, overflowing, organic expression of a gratitude for which God has undeservingly and unfathomably freely given to us, first.

Each of these letting-go statements, mentioned above, are like thick lead-footed concrete bricks. One after another after another, God deliberately, willfully and eagerly picking up with effortless ease and vigorously throwing into the deepest reservoir of His oceans depths (Micah 7:19) as far as the eye can see. One brick at a time being tossed, while making noticeable indents in the white caps of the incoming rushing wave of His raging sea.

Catapulting deep into the darkest deepest pit of the hidden, never-been-visited caves, they dive themselves head first into the muck and mire of the seas bottomless foundation. They are never to be seen, never to be heard and never to be spoken of again (Isaiah 43:25.) And this my sweet friend, yes this, is freedom. And it's found solely here in the treasure of surrender.

However, be on alert. Satan will aggressively begin to convince you he's an experienced professional deep-sea diver who actively threatens to return each and every concrete brick right back where he likes them-on you. Keep this truth tightly woven in the core of your heart, *he's a liar*. His native language is deceit (John 8:44.) Nothing, and I mean nothing he whispers in your precious ear is truth. He cannot touch you, (1 John 45:18) and He will flee from you when you resist his corrupt and craftily carried out game plan (James 4:7.) "Don't be intimidated *in any way* by your enemies. This will be a sign to them that they are going to be destroyed, but that you are going to be saved by God Himself" (Philippians 1:28.) He's a bully, he's an enemy, he's a liar and he's an evil counterfeit. He will do all he can to tell you he's re-written your life story. When in truth, this story of yours, this life-calling, this grandiose design implanted deep while in your mother's womb, authored by the Creator Himself, is infinitely more than all we can ask or imagine, far exceeding that of our greatest expectation (Ephesians 3:20.)

It's time to live the life God has predestined and predesigned for us to live. "For I know the plans I have for you. They are plans for good and not for disaster, to give you a future and a hope" (Jeremiah 29:11.) Surrendering our whole selves into God's mighty hand will enable our mind, body, spirit and soul to be fully equipped and strengthened so that we can be on-guard and stand firm against these destructive, life-sucking enemy decoys which desire nothing more than to advise us down the path of generational ruins. Because, all the while, he's constructively convincing our own heart to believe the lie that our lives are beyond repair. Our circumstances are beyond redemption. Our story is beyond restoration.

And yet, we serve, we are loved, we are sealed, we are protected, we are guided, we are instructed by a personal, intimate, faithful, committed God who's in the business of bringing dead things back to life. Yes, the One True Counselor will always tell us there is hope where there seems to be only despair. There is life where there seems to be no breath. There is joy where there seems to be overwhelming sadness. There is restoration where there seems to be utter destruction. There is surrender where there seems to be no hope. God's specialty is rebuilding the ruins and recreating something that's much more beautiful than what was originally designed.

Dear friend, there is no heart too hard not to be softened. There is no mind too twisted not to be reprogrammed. There is no emotion too damaged not to be rescued. There is no un-forgiveness too deep not to be uprooted. There is no shame too hidden not to be flooded with light. There is no marriage too dead not to brought back to life. There is no fear too dark not to be fully surrendered.

Know this one thing-God adores you. He sings songs of praise over you. He finds pure joy out of making your former rubble into majestic fields of beauty. There is no border, no boundary, no limit to what He is capable of doing. Offer Him your heart and be prepared to experience a life that, "No eye has seen, no ear has heard and no mind has imagined what He has prepared for those who love Him" (1 Corinthians 2:9.) God finds great joy and full satisfaction in making our past mess His current message. *"You will show me the way of life, granting me the joy of your presence and the pleasures of living with you forever" (Psalm 16:11.)*

Together, lets allow the buckets of hail, the torrential rain, the un-drivable flooding, the bolts of lightning, and the earthshaking thunder of the-storms-of-life to supernaturally catapult you and me into the joy filled arms of the Only One who can and **will** deliver the calm after the storm.

Welcome home.

Questions to ponder with God

1. Are you willing and/or ready to walk through the doorway of surrender? If so, write out a prayer to God asking for His Holy Spirit to guide, protect and lead you into His mighty hand of freedom. If not, what is holding you back? Write out a prayer asking for God to reveal the inner places of the heart which resists surrendering this area of your life.

2. Have you received and embraced both the love and forgiveness of God? If so, you now have the active ingredient necessary to forgive and love others. Take time today to write out a prayer asking for Him to empower you with His Spirit to forgive those who have betrayed, hurt, wounded, rejected &/or violated you, from the *overflow* of what He has first given to you.

3. Do you believe God has a story, which exceeds that of your imagination, written over you? Take time today to ask and receive from the Holy Spirit what He has authored and hand-penned for your life.

Scriptures

Matthew 16:24-25

Mark 10:28

Isaiah 64:8

Psalm 37:7

Luke 9:23

Matthew 6:33

Romans 12:2

Philippians 4:13

Romans 12:1

Matthew 7:21

What You're saying to me, God....

_____

_____

_____

_____

_____

_____

_____

_____

_____

_____

_____

_____

_____

_____

_____

My prayer to You, Father....

_____

_____

_____

_____

_____

_____

_____

_____

_____

_____

_____

_____

_____

_____

_____

it is well

CHAPTER 7

SURRENDER = IDENTITY

"Before I formed you in the womb I knew you, before you were born, I set you apart...
Jeremiah 1:5

2008ish was a difficult, trying year. My marriage was on verge of dissipation, my faith was near shipwreck and my unpredictable emotions often left me thoroughly exhausted. What was up was down and what was down was up. I was secretly lost, painfully tired and shamefully broken-and not a clue as to who I was or to whom I belonged.

Yet, through my prone to wander heart, God gently reached directly and fearlessly into the mess, impressing on my heart to allow His Word to read my soul. To sit under His life-giving teachings. To glean from His matchless insight. To draw from His unfailing love. To gather His boundless hope. To obtain His immeasurable wisdom. To receive His Fatherly embrace.

And, as much as I'd normally advise against this, I sat

with the Bible on my lap. Cleansing tears dropping from the overflow of my numerous imperfections onto His unlimited and matchless perfections; all while whispering back to Him that wherever He opens His word, wherever He lands my eyes, this is where I'll camp out and study. Read and Digest. Consume and absorb. Cling and surrender. Obey and trust.

So, I blindly opened it. Having no rhyme or reason to where it opened, I settled in and snuggled up for the long haul. Smack dab in the middle of the Old Testament. I was fascinated by the stories which often involved conquering, defeating and obtaining cities. "*Cities*" began to be a running theme, a continuing thread, a repetitive word God hand-stitched as He breathed life into His healing Word and into my parched heart.

Repeatedly and undeniably, I'd hear Him whisper that I was a city. Each time I read about a city which He cared for, rescued, found, restored, redeemed, rebuilt, provided, protected, Fathered, adopted—He was referring to the city of my heart. And although the orphan heart within was unsettled, wounded, fractured and divided, this I knew with every fiber of my being; He was sharing my new identity. I was His *city*, and He was rebuilding the ruins.

The word *city* soon took on an entirely new influential meaning in those early days of healing, and I began to find myself waking up before the 5:00 a.m. alarm to receive His instruction hand chiseled deep within the city walls of the heart. But it wasn't until a February afternoon while pulling into a California parking lot, I fully understood the impactful meaning and the life-altering definition of the word, *city*.

It was on this particular car ride where satan sat shot gun and aggressively exposed all my fears. Disclosed all my failures. Unconcealed all my deficiencies. Bared all my shame. Displayed all my regret. All. The new identity I had been receiving through God's word of being His city, a city for which He cared, loved and promised to restore, was now strategically replaced with the enemy's convincing lie that I had done too much. Wandered too far. Sinned too often. Yep, it was simply too late for this orphan, I heard loudly and crystal clear that February afternoon.

No longer being able to drive, I pulled into the nearest driveway of a store parking lot. Struggling to put the car in park, I placed my head back on the head rest and experienced a washing-over of intense hopelessness. "Maybe it is too late for me. Maybe God doesn't give second, third, fourth and beyond chances. Maybe this time, He's done rescuing me. Maybe this time, I've worn Him out. Maybe this time, I've exhausted His grace. Maybe this time..." I began to repeat and believe.

And without the slightest hint of hesitation, as if this were out of a meticulous movie scene, the song "God of This City" rung loudly through the car speakers, piercing straight into the ears of my conflicted heart. Immediately the word "city" sung like an angel hand delivering me a divine gift of perfectly timed *hope*, while my thoughts unhesitatingly drifted from satan's destructive words and now fastened themselves onto God's truth of my identity through the gift of this new song.

"For greater things have yet to come,
*And greater things are <u>still</u> to be done in **this city.***
Greater things have yet to come,
*And greater things are <u>still</u> to be done in **this city.***

There in no one like our God.
There is no one like our God.

For greater things are yet to come,
*And greater things are <u>still</u> to be done in **this city**."*

The chorus repeated and repeated and repeated ... until God received my full attention and positioned my heart to look up and secure His make-no-sense grace while effortlessly responding in return, "I hear you, Father. It's not over for me. It's not too late. In fact, it's just begun. My identity is found only in You and nothing of the past, current or future is wasted. Nothing. Greater things have yet to come and greater things are still to be done, *in this city."*

Grace. It's a beautiful gift, isn't it? An inexhaustible gift. In the muck of exhaustion, in the quicksand of brokenness, in the flooding waters of relational chaos, in the web of negative thinking, in the fog of identity-crisis, in the pit of despair, grace shines its radiating light onto tomorrow's resurrection through the unfathomable gift of surrender.

You can be assured of this precious sister, God speaks this truth directly into your loved and adopted heart while in the presence of the enemy of your soul, moment by moment:

"I turn your deserts into pools of water, the dry land into springs of water. I bring the hungry to settle there and build their city.

They sow their fields, plant their vineyards,

and harvest their bumper crops.

How I bless them"

(Psalm 107 35-3.)

"I, The Lord will guide you continually, giving you

water when you are dry and restoring your strength.

You will be like a well-watered garden,

like an ever-flowing spring.

Some of you will rebuild the

deserted ruins of your cities.

Then you will be known as a rebuilder

of walls and a restorer of homes."

(Isaiah 58 11-12.)

His Love eradicates the paralyzing shame which has imprisoned us from our true authentic self. His Love erases the yoke of guilt which has blocked intimacy with God and others. His Love heals the tormenting fear which has prevented us from seeking our purpose, our calling, our mission, our destination.

His active ingredient of love is the true remedy to all things broken- including our own identity. Ephesians 3:19 shares the key to life: "May you experience the love of Christ, though it's too great to fully understand. **Then**= you will be made complete with all the fullness of life and power that comes from God." Experiencing the very essence of His love, according to God's Word, says we are made complete and full of both life and power! That is why, dear friend, at the root, at the core, at the very deepest belief system of the heart, our identity flows out only from the knowing, the receiving, the experiencing of His love.

Since our beliefs often usher in our thoughts, and our thoughts usher in our feelings, and our feelings usher in our behaviors; (**beliefs=thoughts=feelings=behaviors**) then it's clear that if our current belief is that we are loved by God (not based off of anything but His undeserved grace,) thoughts of worthiness, feelings of joy and behaviors of trust naturally begin to emerge. On the other hand, the opposite also holds true. If our belief is that we are un-loveable, un-forgivable, un-restorable; thoughts of unworthiness, feelings of despair and behaviors of an orphan mentality will begin to materialize. It begins and ends with LOVE.

Don't be fooled, loved one. Satan will work overtime to destroy that which God has done in you, through the power, perfection and might of His all sufficient love. You see, satan has already read your God-designed story and knows the generational, immeasurable, beautiful calling God has announced, declared and proclaimed over your life. And it's his greatest objective to deceive your precious, adopted and loved heart into believing it's simply not worth living out. But let me just remind you, it is precious one. It is.

Satan will inevitably speak **<u>facts</u>** in a desperate effort to prevent us from embracing our identity; while God, on the other hand, will speak **Truth** (John 16:13.)

Facts will say: You've sinned too much, too often, too frequent.
Truth will say: "I will make your sins as white as snow. Though they're as red as crimson, I will make them as white and pure as wool" (Isaiah 1:18.)

Facts will say: You're not enough.
Truth will say: "My grace is sufficient for you, for my power is made perfect in weakness" (2 Corinthians 12:9.)

Facts will say: You're not loved.
Truth will say: "My love has been poured into your heart through the Holy Spirit" (Romans 5:5.)

Facts will say: This task is too difficult.
Truth will say: "Humanly speaking, it is impossible. But with God everything is possible" (Matthew 19:26.)

Facts will say: This marriage is dead.
Truth will say: "Abraham believed in the God who brings the dead back to life and who creates new things out of nothing" (Romans 4:17.)

Facts will say: I'm invisible.
Truth will say: "I know you by name" (John 10:3.)

Facts will say: This situation is hopeless.

Truth will say: "But those who trust in the Lord for help will find their strength renewed. They will run and not grow weary; they will walk and not grow weak" (Isaiah 40:31.)

Because the One who says you are whole and healed (Isaiah 53:5) also says:

You are forgiven (1 John 1:9)
You are His masterpiece (Ephesians 2:10)
You are firmly rooted (Colossians 2:7)
You are redeemed (Isaiah 43:1)
You are restored (Jeremiah 30:17)
You are His workmanship (Ephesians. 2:10)
You are an overcomer (Revelation 12:11)
You are His child (1 Peter 1:23)
You are His joint-heir (Romans 8:17)
You are a conqueror (Romans 8:27)
You are holy and blameless (Colossians. 1:22)
You are complete in Him (Colossians 2:10)
You have no lack (Psalm 34:18)
You have the power of God (Ephesians 1:19)
You have the spirit of wisdom (Ephesians 1:17)
You have the righteousness of Christ (Romans 3:22)
You have a sound mind (2 Timothy 1:7)
You can do all things through Him (Philippians 4:13)
You are His vessel (2 timothy 2:21)
You are loved (Nehemiah 9:17)
He will never fail you (Deuteronomy 31:8)
He can't forget you (Isaiah 49:15
He will fight for you (Exodus 14:14)
He will search for you (Jeremiah 29:13)

He sings songs of victory over you (Psalm 32:7)
He delights in you (Zephaniah 3:17)
He will never abandon you (Psalm 27:10)
He will strengthen you (Colossians 1:11)
He will be with you (Isaiah 43:2)

Soak that in.

Because they're for you. Not just her, not just him, not just someone else more deserving. For you, beautiful one. It's here where our identity, our purpose, our worth, our very calling will be something we work from and not for-enabling our anchored heart to radiate authenticity and confident hope for that which He has sown deep in the core of our being. God simply says to, "Ask me and I will tell you remarkable secrets you do not know about things to come" (Jeremiah 33:3.) The One who has remarkable secrets hidden away just-for-you, also:

adores you.

Loves you.

Longs for you.

Waits for you.

Our brokenness never scares Him, it draws Him.

Our weakness never repulses Him, it touches Him.

Our fragility never worries Him, it reveals Him.

We'll find God not sitting amongst the great, but walking intently with His beautifully broken, abundantly loved and plentifully cherished warriors. Warriors brave enough to resist the sitting position with the great for a humble hike on the rocky path of life-being carried and led by the only Light potent enough to reveal the hope of tomorrow. All with one foot print at a time, in the security and knowledge of who we are and to whom we belong.

As we draw to a close on this journey together- falling north into our Papa's mighty hands together, I know that my eyes may have never locked with yours. My path may have never crossed yours. But I know something about you. You haven't done too much. You haven't wandered too far. You haven't strayed too many times. You haven't fallen too hard. You haven't messed up too deep- for Your Maker, Your Creator, Your Father to not relentlessly, intently, joyfully, passionately and limitlessly rush to your aid and administer forgiveness, and healing, and grace, and love, and kindness, and *rest* into the former dry land of your beautiful *city.* Your very identity.

You are a city on a hill that cannot be hidden, denied, unloved, forgotten, rejected, left and/or lost. You, beloved, are the light of the world (Matthew 5:14.) Greater things have yet to come, greater things are still to be done, *in your city.*

"For I know the plans I have for you, declares the Lord, plans to prosper you and not to harm you, plans to give you a hop and a future."
Jeremiah 29:11

Questions to ponder

1. Write out your own fact vs. Truth list below:

2. What surprised you about this list? What did God reveal to you while writing this list?

3. In a time of solitude and quietness, ask the Holy Spirit to reveal any and all areas where His Spirit may be quenched, resulting in a lack knowing, receiving and experiencing both His love and His adoption status. Give these areas over to Him to be crucified and nailed to His cross so that His river of Life-giving water can fill in every empty place of the heart.

Scriptures

Ephesians 1:5

1 John 3:1

John 15:5

Ephesians 2:10

2 Corinthians 1:21-22

<u>Isaiah 43:1</u>

<u>Romans 8:16</u>

<u>Jeremiah 1:5</u>

What You're saying to me, God....

_____

_____

_____

_____

_____

_____

_____

_____

_____

_____

_____

_____

_____

_____

_____

My prayer to You, Father....

_____

_____

_____

_____

_____

_____

_____

_____

_____

_____

_____

_____

_____

_____

Cast all your
anxiety on Him
because he cares
for you
1 Peter 5:7

CPSIA information can be obtained
at www.ICGtesting.com
Printed in the USA
BVHW041841100920
588575BV00014B/640